**Invasi**

**A T**

By ~~Maria Novi~~

*methuen* | drama
LONDON • NEW YORK • OXFORD • NEW DELHI • SYDNEY

METHUEN DRAMA
Bloomsbury Publishing Plc 50 Bedford Square, London, WC1B 3DP, UK
Bloomsbury Publishing Inc, 1359 Broadway, New York, NY 10018, USA
Bloomsbury Publishing Ireland, 29 Earlsfort Terrace, Dublin 2, D02 AY28, Ireland

BLOOMSBURY, METHUEN DRAMA and the Methuen
Drama logo are trademarks of Bloomsbury Publishing Plc

First published in Great Britain 2025

Copyright © Maia Novi, 2025

Maia Novi has asserted her right under the Copyright, Designs
and Patents Act, 1988, to be identified as author of this work.

For legal purposes the Acknowledgements on p. vii constitute
an extension of this copyright page.

Front cover image/design by Victoria Del SelBack
Cover image by David Goddard

All rights reserved. No part of this publication may be: i) reproduced or
transmitted in any form, electronic or mechanical, including photocopying, recording
or by means of any information storage or retrieval system without prior permission
in writing from the publishers; or ii) used or reproduced in any way for the training,
development or operation of artificial intelligence (AI) technologies, including
generative AI technologies. The rights holders expressly reserve this publication
from the text and data mining exception as per Article 4(3) of the
Digital Single Market Directive (EU) 2019/790.

Bloomsbury Publishing Plc does not have any control over, or responsibility for,
any third-party websites referred to or in this book. All internet addresses given
in this book were correct at the time of going to press. The author and publisher
regret any inconvenience caused if addresses have changed or sites have
ceased to exist, but can accept no responsibility for any such changes.

No rights in incidental music or songs contained in the work are hereby granted
and performance rights for any performance/presentation whatsoever
must be obtained from the respective copyright owners.

All rights whatsoever in this play are strictly reserved and application for
performance etc. should be made before rehearsals to Linden Entertainment.
No performance may be given unless a licence has been obtained

A catalogue record for this book is available from the British Library.

Library of Congress Control Number: 2025944502

ISBN: PB: 978-1-3506-0221-2
ePDF: 978-1-3506-0222-9
eBook: 978-1-3506-0223-6

Series: Modern Plays

Typeset by Westchester Publishing Services
Printed and bound in Great Britain

For product safety related questions contact productsafety@bloomsbury.com.

To find out more about our authors and books visit
www.bloomsbury.com and sign up for our newsletters.

# Invasive Species

By Maia Novi

Directed and developed by Michael Breslin

## UK Cast And Creative Team

| | |
|---|---|
| Maia | **Maia Novi** |
| Performer 2 | **Kalifa Taylor** |
| Performer 3 | **Harrison Osterfield** |
| Performer 4 | **Max Percy** |
| Performer 5 | **Ella Blackburn** |
| | |
| Writer | **Maia Novi** |
| Director | **Michael Breslin** |
| Dramaturg | **Amauta Marston-Firmino** |
| Casting Director | **Sarah-Jane Price** |
| UK Set & Costume Designer | **Damien Stanton** |
| UK Associate Lighting Designer | **Ben Jacobs** |
| UK Associate Sound Designer | **Dominic Brennan** |
| Movement Director | **Beth Gill** |
| Company Stage Manager | **Alexandra Kataigida** |
| Production Manager | **Carrie Croft** |
| General Manager | **James Quaife** |
| Assistant Director | **Maxi Himpe** |
| Costume Supervisor | **Charlie Rowan** |
| Originating Set & Costume Designer | **Cole McCarty** |
| Originating Lighting Designer | **Yichen Zhou** |
| Originating Sound Designer | **Maxwell Neely-Cohen & Jessie Char** |
| | |
| Producers | **Eric Kuhn Productions & Adam Rodner** |
| Co-producers | **Lucy Moss, Salem Productions, Amplify Pictures, John Voege, Amauta M. Firmino, Maria Ines Olmedo** |
| Executive Producer | **James Quaife** |

| | |
|---|---|
| Marketing | **Cup of Ambition** |
| PR | **Kate Morley PR** |
| Creative Direction | **Invasive Studios** |
| Graphic Design | **Martin Naranjo** |
| Production Accounting Consultancy | **Deus Ex Machina Productions** |
| Photographer | **Victoria Del Sel** |
| Video Shoot Director | **Eduardo Braun** |
| Video Production Designer | **Ambar Mallmann** |
| Video Director of Photography | **Enzo Cedar** |
| Video Producer | **Sonia Stigliano** |
| Insurance | **Gordon & Co** |
| Marketing Intern | **Taylor Emerson** |

# Cast

### Maia

**Maia Novi** is a writer and actor based in NYC, her play *Invasive Species* was named one of the "Top 10 Cultural Events of 2024" by the *Hollywood Reporter*. Her recent acting credits include *5 Models in Ruins, 1981* at the Lincoln Center and *Invasive Species* at the Vineyard's Dimson Theatre. She is currently developing her first feature with Film4.

IG: @maianovi

### Performer 2

**Kalifa Taylor** is a native British actor who was nominated for an Off West End (Offie) Award for her performance as Helena in *All's Well That Ends Well*. Other performances include: *Noises Off!* (Theatre Royal Haymarket), *All's Well That Ends Well* (Shakespeare in the Squares), *A Christmas Carol: A Ghost Story* (Birmingham Rep), *Taming of the Shrew* (Shakespeare in the Squares), *Look Who's All Grown Up* (The Space), *Selected Recordings of Us* (Space Theatre), *Money Heist: The Experience* (Fever), *Tomb King* (The League of Adventure), *The Gunpowder Plot Immersive Experience* (Historic Royal Palaces and Layered Reality), *Hamlet* (Southwark Playhouse), *War Inside* (Vault Festival), *Laura and Sophia* (Lion & Unicorn Theatre), *Feel More X Lately* (Lion & Unicorn Theatre), *1000 Ways the World Will End (& How It Starts Again)* (King's Head Theatre).

### Performer 3

**Harrison Osterfield** is a UK-based British actor who first gained prominence through his supporting role as *Snowden* in the Hulu war drama mini-series *Catch-22*. His role was met with high praise from George Clooney, who served as executive producer on the project. Premiering in 2021, Harrison starred as a series lead, Leopold, in the Netflix mystery adventure crime drama series *The Irregulars*. Harrison attended The BRIT School and was later accepted at the London Academy of Music and Dramatic Art. Harrison most recently wrapped on WW2 feature film *Pressure* opposite Andrew Scott.

## Performer 4

**Max Percy** is a multi-disciplinary artist creating across theatre, dance and technology. Recent work includes *Baklâ* (Asian Arts Award Winner 2023), *This is Not a Show about Hong Kong* (Untapped Award Winner & *Scotsman*'s Fringe First 2022). He developed the creative technology project "Convergence" with Mediale, Glasshouse International Centre for Music, and "Technology to make Dance more Accessible for Blind and Partially Sighted" with East London Dance and the London College of Fashion, published by the International Conference of Movement and Computing, Chicago 2022. He is Co-Artistic Director of Papergang Theatre, Artistic Associate at Roots Touring and New Earth Theatre, and a member of the cabaret supergroup, Dragon Boiz.

## Performer 5

**Ella Blackburn** is originally from Teesdale in County Durham. She trained at Royal Central School of Speech and Drama. Recent theatre credits include *Julius Caesar* (Orange Tree Theatre), *Macbeth* (Young Shakespeare Company), *The Merchant of Venice* (OVO Theatre), *Much Ado About Nothing* (Oddsocks), and *Windfall* (Southwark Playhouse). She recently wrapped the short film *Monkey* for Silas Productions.

# Creative Team

### MICHAEL BRESLIN  Director

Michael Breslin is a Pulitzer Prize finalist who writes and directs plays, musicals, and movies. His musical *The Last Bimbo of the Apocalypse* was named a NYT Critics's Pick and "the best musical to date about living online" (Ben Brantley). Other projects include: *The Wives* (film in development with A24 + Apple), *Circle Jerk* (Obie Award), *This American Wife*, *Ratatouille the TikTok Musical,* and *Invasive Species.* He holds his doctorate and MFA from Yale School of Drama.

### AMAUTA MARSTON-FIRMINO  Dramaturg

Amauta M. Firmino is a New York-based writer, producer, and dramaturg. He was the production dramaturg on Broadway's *Slave Play* and recently produced and dramaturged *Invasive Species* at the Vineyard's Dimson Theatre. Recent credits include: *Spirit of the People* (Williamstown Theatre Festival), and *Dilaria* (DR2 Theatre). He has developed new plays at the Yale Repertory Theatre, New York Theatre Workshop, Playwrights Horizons, Lincoln Center Theater, the Kennedy Center, and the Sundance Theatre Labs.

### SARAH-JANE PRICE  Casting Director

Recipient of the 2025 WhatsOnStage Award for Best Casting Direction for Olivier Nominated *Why Am I So Single?*

Theatre includes: *Charlie and The Chocolate Factory* (Europe), *Invasive Species* (King's Head Theatre), *The Turning* (New Musical Workshop), *Why am I So Single?* (Garrick Theatre), *Midnight Cowboy* (Southwark Playhouse), *Madagascar* (UK Tour, International Tour), *Pop Off, Michelangelo!* (London and Edinburgh), *For Tonight* (Adelphi Theatre), *Starry* (Ameena Hamid Productions), *The Hijabi Monologues* (Bush Theatre), *White Rabbit, Red Rabbit* (Bush Theatre), *Fame* (London and UK Tour), *Little Miss Sunshine* (Arcola Theatre and UK Tour), *Trompe L'oeil* (The Other Palace), *Bring it On* (Royal Festival Hall), *The Adding Machine* (Finborough Theatre), *Mr Men and Little Miss* (Edinburgh / Underbelly), *Frankenstein* (UK Tour), *Treasure Island* (The Barn Theatre).

Sarah-Jane also cast a retrospective season of work at the Bush Theatre and Immersion Theatre's inaugural and current season. She was Head of Casting at TED Entertainment and is Casting Consultant on concert productions of *Evita, Love Never Dies, Bonnie and Clyde, The Light Princess*, and more.

Her most recent credits are *A Christmas Carol-ish* (Soho Place), *Pop Off, Michelangelo!* (London), *Mayä the Musical* (London Workshop), *Something Rotten* and *Oklahoma!* in Concert (Theatre Royal Drury Lane), *We Aren't Kids Anymore* (The Savoy Theatre), Casting Director on Oxford Playhouse projects and Casting Associate on the brand new musical *Burlesque* in Manchester.

## **DAMIEN STANTON**  UK Set & Costume Designer

Damien is a London-based designer working across stage, events, and installations.

He was Set Designer on *Brainiac Live* at the Marylebone Theatre, which won the 2025 Olivier Award for Best Family Show.

Recent design credits include: *Jamie Allan's Amaze* (New World Stages, NYC), *Bury The Hatchet* (Pleasance Queen Dome), *Machinal* (Mountview), *Transport Explorers* (London Transport Museum), *The Acts* (Barbican), *Jamie Allan's Amaze* (Criterion Theatre), *Wonderland in Alice* (Octagon Theatre), *Brainiac Live* (Marylebone Theatre), *Hamstrung* (Omnibus Theatre & Pleasance), the *Spectrum Roundel Installation* (Transport for London), *Stephen Mulhern – Beyond Belief* (UK Tour), *Brainiac Live* (Dubai Opera House), the *Poster Chandelier* (London Transport Museum), *Paddington™ LoComotion* (Blenheim Palace), *Peter Rabbit™ Easter Adventure* (Covent Garden), and *Peter Rabbit™ Garden Adventure* (Blenheim Palace).

Associate design credits include *The Yellow Wallpaper* (Sadler's Wells & Czech National Theatre) and *Lisbon Floor* (Copenhagen Opera Festival).

Damien received *The Stage Award for Innovation in Theatre* and was named in *The Stage 100* for co-founding and running Theatre Support Fund+ during the COVID-19 pandemic. The campaign, *The Show Must Go On!*, raised over £1 million to support theatre workers facing financial hardship.

He is passionate about championing the work of Neurodivergent artists and creatives living with Neurological Disabilities, and advocating for greater awareness, access, and visibility across the industry.

## **BEN JACOBS** UK Associate Lighting Designer

Trained in Lighting Design at the Royal Central School of Speech and Drama in London.

Credits include: *Oliver!* (Chichester Festival Theatre & West End), *Dawn French is a Huge Twat* (UK Tour & West End), *Miss Julie, King Hamlin* (Park Theatre), *Evita* (Parque Villa-Lobos, Sau Paulo), *Singing in the Rain* (Teatro Sergio Cardoso, Sao Paulo), *Saving Mozart,* (The Other Palace), *1984* (Hackney Town Hall), *Salome, Seussical, Bring it On* (Southwark Playhouse), *Brenda's Got a Baby* (New Diorama Theatre), *A Midsummer Night's Dream* (Wilton's Music Hall), *Caterpillar* (Stephen Joseph Theatre), *The Sorrows of Satan* (Brocket Hall), *The Retreat, Dolphins & Sharks, Melting Pot, Maggie & Pierre* (Finborough Theatre), *NoMad, Lord of the Flies, Edward II* (Greenwich Theatre), *Nora: A Doll's House, H.R.Aitch, Heartbreak House, Carmen, Twang, Privates on Parade, Imagine This* (The Union Theatre), *Midlife Cowboy, Freefall* (Pleasance Theatre), *Sister* (Ovalhouse), *People We Didn't Quite Meet, Red, Are We Stronger Than Winston* (The Place), *Proud, Southern Belles, Stripped, The Stones* (King's Head Theatre), *One Giant Leap, Gentleman Jack, Taro, Precious Little, The White Rose, Kes, Golden F\*\*king Years, Three Sisters, Dracula, Cinderella, Macbeth, The State of Things, Frankenstein, Wolves of Willoughby Chase, Side by Side by Sondheim, Jack Studio Theatre. Caterpillar, In Event of Moone Disaster, The State We're In, Elexion, Red Like Embers* (Theatre 503), *Adam & Eve, Foul Pages* (The Hope Theatre), *The Lower Depths, Hamlet, Burial at Thebes, Love & Information, Secret Circus* (RCSSD), *Cuncrete, Mrs Armitage and the Big Wave* (UK Tour), *Jamaica Inn, I Love my Love, The Lost Happy Endings, Fanny & Faggot* (Tabard Theatre), Macbeth (Bussey Building), *Lunatic, The League of Youth* (Theatre N16).

Associate Lighting Designer credits include: *Les Misérables* (UK Tour/West End/International), *Fiddler on the Roof* (Regent's Park), *Dear England* (National Theatre & West End), *The Motive and the Cue* (Noel Coward Theatre), *Anna* (National Theatre, Dorfman), *Le Nozze di Figaro* (Glyndebourne), *Sondheim's Old Friends*

(Sondheim Theatre & Gielgud Theatre), *Ostalgie* (National Theatre Studio), *Project O* (Southbank Centre), *Crave* (Prague Quadrennial).

Ben was the recipient of the Olivier Award for Best Lighting Design in 2025, and has been nominated for the Off West End Award for Best Lighting Design four times, winning the award in 2018 and 2022.

### **DOMINIC BRENNAN** UK Associate Sound Designer

Dominic Brennan is a composer and sound designer from West London. Previous shows include: *Lost Watches* (Park Theatre), *The Gang of Three* (King's Head Theatre), *Surrender* (Arcola Theatre), *The Children* (Nottingham Playhouse), *The Misandrist* (Arcola Theatre), *STRIKE!* (Southwark Playhouse), *Mediocre White Male* (Park Theatre), *Shackleton and his Stowaway* (Park Theatre), *Spiderfly* (Theatre 503), *We're Staying Right Here* (Park Theatre), *Cuckoo* (Soho Theatre) and *The Universal Machine* (New Diorama Theatre). In 2017 he won the Off-West End Award for Sound Design for his work on *Down & Out in Paris and London* (New Diorama Theatre). Other work includes music for adverts, short films and a sound installation at the Princess of Wales Conservatory in Kew Gardens.

### **BETH GILL** Movement Director

Beth Gill is an award-winning choreographer based in New York City since 2025. Her multidisciplinary works are captivating, cinematic timescales, the product of long-term collaborations with celebrated artists. Gill is the proud recipient of the Hern Alpert, Doris Duke Impact, Foundation for Contemporary Art and "Bessie" awards. She has toured nationally and internationally and been honoured with a Guggenheim Fellowship, NEFA's National Dance Project grant, Princeton's Hodder Fellowship and Lower Manhattan Cultural Council's Extended Life Artist in Residence.

### **CARRIE CROFT** Production Manager

Carrie is a Production Manager, Producer and General Manager, based in London and working in both off-West End and West End theatres. She completed the MA Collaborative Theatre Production and Design course at Guildhall School of Music and Drama with Distinction in 2022.

Recent theatre productions include: *Lost Watches and Conversations After Sex* (Park Theatre), *Stalled* (Kings Head Theatre), *10 Nights* (National Tour), *Cinderella* (Queens Theatre Hornchurch), *Bombay Superstars* (West End and Tour), *Echo and Narcissus* and *Deep Blue Sea* (Theatre Royal Bath, Ustinov), *Julie: The Musical* (The Other Palace), *Priscilla the Party* (West End), *Foam* (Finborough Theatre), *Othello* (Riverside Studios), *Birthright* (Finborough Theatre), *Disruption and Shape of Things* (Park Theatre), *Rocky Horror 50th Anniversary Gala* (West End), *Fucking Men* (Waterloo East), *Breeding* (King's Head Theatre), *Under the Black Rock* (Arcola Theatre), *Sus* (Park 90, Park Theatre).

**JAMES QUAIFE** General Manager & Executive Producer

As co-producer: *Retrograde* (Apollo Theatre, West End), *Kiss Me Kate* (Barbican Theatre), the Olivier Nominated *A Strange Loop* (Barbican Theatre) and *A Little Life* (Richmond Theatre, Harold Pinter, Savoy Theatre, West End).

Productions include: *Jack and the Beanstalk*, *Invasive Species*, *The Pitchfork Disney*, *The Gang of Three, Cinderella* and *Buyer & Cellar* (King's Head Theatre), Steven Bartlett's *The Diary of a CEO Live* (The London Palladium, UK & Ireland Tour), *Captain Sandy Live* (UK Tour, Duchess Theatre & Lyric Theatre, West End), *Antics With Ash* (Reading & Leeds Festival), *There's No Place Like Home* (Lyric Theatre, West End), *Khiyon Hursey in Concert* (The Other Palace), *Alyssa, Memoirs of a Queen* and *Legends of Lockdown Live* (Vaudeville Theatre, West End), *Sweat* (Gielgud Theatre; Winner of the *Evening Standard* Award for Best Play 2019 and Olivier Nominated for Best New Play), *Good People* starring Imelda Staunton (Noël Coward Theatre), *Barking in Essex* starring Lee Evans, Sheila Hancock and Keeley Hawes (Wyndham's Theatre; *Evening Standard* and WhatsOnStage Award nominations for Best New Comedy), *Next Fall* (Southwark Playhouse), *Step 9 (of 12)* and *Precious Little Talent* (Trafalgar Studios).

From 2014–2019 James was the producer for English Touring Theatre where he produced and general managed over 15 UK tours, including the West End transfer of *Equus* (Trafalgar Studios/Theatre Royal Stratford East/UK tour; Winner of the UK Theatre Awards, Best Revival 2019 & the Off-West End Awards for Best Production 2019).

James is a member of The Society of London Theatre and a Trustee for the King's Head Theatre. @jamesquaife | jamesquaifeproductions.com | newframeproductions.com

## **COLE MCCARTY** Originating Set & Costume Designer

Cole McCarty is a costume designer based in NYC. He is a key collaborator for the theatre company Fake Friends, collaborating on all their workshops/productions, including the Pulitzer Prize-nominated *Circle Jerk* and their most recent project, *The Last Bimbo of the Apocalypse*. His film work has been seen at various festivals, including the Sundance Film Festival, the Switzerland International Film Festival, and the Amsterdam International Film Festival.

Selected venues: Two River Theater, Portland Stage Company, The Vineyard Theatre, Williamstown Theatre Festival, Dallas Theater Center, The New Group.

Faculty: Meadows School of the Arts and Fashion Institute of Technology, New York

MFA: Yale School of Drama

## **YICHEN ZHOU** Originating Lighting Designer

Yichen Zhou is a theatre designer working mostly with lighting and scenery. Recent credits include: *Invasive Species* (Vineyard Theatre), *Vile Isle* (The Tank), *Faust* (Heartbeat Opera), *The Return of Benjamin Lay* (The Sheen Center, The Sedgwick Theatre), *Your Name Means Dream* (TheaterWorks Hartford), *Kin* (Chain Theatre), *The Woman in Black* (Weston Theatre Company), *The Far Country* (Yale Rep), *The Rasa Project* (National Sawdust), *The Life and Death of King John* (Juilliard School), *National Playwrights Conference* (The O'Neill).

Website: www.zhouyichen.design

## **JESSIE CHAR & MAXWELL NEELY-COHEN** Originating Sound Designer

Jessie and Maxwell's work has spanned theater, video games, film, literature, and dance. Jessie is a cellist, designer, programmer, and composer. She founded the LAYERS design conference and the Pacific Helm design agency. Maxwell is a writer, musician, and software artist.

He is a consulting dramaturg for the New York Choreographic Institute at New York City Ballet and a Fellow at the Library Innovation Lab at Harvard Law School.

## Producers

### ERIC KUHN PRODUCTIONS  Producer

Eric Kuhn Productions is a production company bridging entertainment between London and New York. It is led by Eric Kuhn, a theatre, documentary, film, and TV show producer, whose work has won numerous awards and accolades including three Tony Awards, a Peabody, two GLAAD awards, and a British Independent Film Award (BIFA).

In London, Kuhn's credits include *Born with Teeth* (Wyndham's Theatre), *The Frogs* (Southwark Playhouse), *The Unfriend* (Criterion & Wyndham's Theatre), and *Accidental Death of an Anarchist* (Haymarket Theatre).

His Broadway credits include *Shucked, Life of Pi, A Strange Loop* (2022 Tony Award), *Is This A Room, Dana H., The Inheritance* (2020 Tony Award), *Rodgers & Hammerstein's Oklahoma!* (2019 Tony Award) and *Harvey Fierstein's Torch Song Trilogy*. Off-Broadway, he has produced *Invasive Species* (Vineyard's Dimson Theatre), *Danny and the Deep Blue Sea* (Lucille Lortel Theatre), and *This Beautiful Future* (Cherry Lane Theatre).

Eric is an executive producer of the feature documentary *Grand Theft Hamlet*, which won three international film festivals (including the South by Southwest Grand Jury Award for Best Documentary Feature), two BIFAs, was long listed for a BAFTA, and is now streaming on MUBI. He is also an Executive Producer behind the documentary *We Are Pat* (world premiere at 2025 Tribeca Film Festival). Kuhn's first feature film, *ISH*, is backed by the BBC and the British Film Institute (BFI) and premiered at the 2025 Venice Film Festival's Critics' Week.

He also serves on the board of New York Stage and Film, where he previously was the Executive Producer, and on the advisory committee of the American Theatre Wing.

IG: @EricJKuhn

## ADAM RODNER  Producer

Adam Rodner is a producer working across theater, film, TV, and dance. Select Broadway lead producing work includes *To Kill a Mockingbird* (Broadway; London; N.A Tour), *The Lehman Trilogy, West Side Story, Gary: A Sequel to Titus Andronicus, King Lear, Hillary & Clinton, Who's Afraid of Virginia Woolf? The Waverly Gallery, The Music Man*. Associate: *Book of Mormon* (Broadway; N.A. Tour; UK Tour), *Hello, Dolly!* (N.A. Tour). Recent: *Second Acts Live* (N.A. Tour); *Invasive Species* (Vineyard; King's Head Theatre), *Other People's Dead Dads* (Dixon Place), *xXPonyBoyDerekXx* (OnlyFans), *Looking for Papa* (Cherry Lane Theatre). Film & TV work and development includes *What We Do in The Shadows* (FX Networks), *Devs* (FX Networks), *mid90s* (A24), *The Tragedy of Macbeth* (A24), *Past Lives* (A24), *Uncut Gems* (A24), *Diagnosis* (Netflix), *Barkskins* (NatGeo). Awards include Tony Award Nomination for Best Play (*Gary*), three Clio Awards for integrated advertising achievement, Drama Desk Award, and an Outer Critics Circle Honor. He has developed productions with Adam Guettel, LaTanya Richardson Jackson, Justin Peck, Jeremy O. Harris, Dustin Wills, Craig Lucas, Jaki Bradley, Annie Hamilton, and Miranda Haymon, among others. Adam has a BFA in Dramatic Writing from NYU Tisch School of the Arts, where he studied under playwrights Richard Wesley and Francine Volpe.

## Co-Producers

### LUCY MOSS  Co-producer

Lucy is a Tony Award-winning writer and the youngest woman ever to direct a musical on Broadway (lol). Alongside her co-writer/friend, Toby Marlow, she won a Tony Award, two Drama Desks, and an Outer Critics Circle Award for their music and lyrics in the musical *SIX* (Broadway, West End, various other cool places). Their album *SIX: Live on Opening Night* was also nominated for a Grammy. She was ALSO nominated for best director of a musical at the Tony's for her co-direction of *SIX*.

Okay enough about *SIX*. Other writer-director credits include *Why Am I So Single?* (West End), *Hot Gay Time Machine* (West End).

Her directing credits include: *Legally Blonde* (Regent's Park Open Air Theatre), *Ratatouille: The TikTok Musical* (Actors' Fund Online Benefit).

Her song-writing credits include: *The Monkey King* (Netflix), *Book of Queer* (discovery+), *The 75th Annual Tony Awards* (CBS), and the upcoming *Bad Fairies* (Locksmith/Warner Bros).

She loves to kayak. You can find her on the internet @mucyloss.

## SALEM PRODUCTIONS  Co-Producer

Salem Productions, led by Elizabeth Salem, is thrilled to celebrate its first birthday with Maia Novi's dark comedy *Invasive Species*. This NYC-based production company has proudly contributed as co-producer or investor to a range of acclaimed productions, including Broadway's *Operation Mincemeat* (Tony-nominated for Best Musical), *Maybe Happy Ending*, *The Last Five Years*, the upcoming *Chess* and *Queen of Versailles*, as well as Off-Broadway's *25th Annual Putnam County Spelling Bee*.

In London's West End, it recently co-produced the sold-out presentation of *Little Dancer* at Theatre Royal Drury Lane, and is a proud investor in the Olivier-winning *Fiddler on the Roof*, *Good Night, Oscar* and *The Producers*. While honored to be part of these celebrated productions, their mission and focus is on creating new work and championing emerging voices. To that end, the company is co-producing *Lewis Loves Clark*, a new musical by Dylan MarcAurele and Mike Ross; has commissioned a new play from Shirley Jackson Award–winning writer Robert Shearman; and is co-producing the upcoming film *Our Dead Dead Drug Lord*, based on Alexis Scheer's critically praised Off-Broadway play.

To learn more, visit salemproductions.com.

## AMPLIFY PICTURES  Co-Producer

Amplify Pictures is an independent studio founded by Emmy and Tony winner Joe Lewis (*Fleabag, Transparent*). Their first Tony nomination was *Gutenberg! The Musical!* and they recently co-produced Dilaria Off-Broadway. Season three of their Emmy-winning docuseries, *100 Foot Wave*, is on HBO MAX. Their Sundance award-winning documentary feature *Come See Me in the Good Light*, directed by Ryan White about the late poet Andrea Gibson, will be released on Apple TV+ in the fall.

IG: @amplifypics

## JOHN VOEGE  Co-Producer

John Voege is thrilled to be making his London theatre debut as co-producer of *Invasive Species*. A life-long theatre enthusiast, John serves on the Advisory Committee of the American Theatre Wing and is a trustee on the board of Goodspeed Musicals (East Haddam, Connecticut). He also serves as trustee of The Case Graber Foundation, supporting performing arts. Upcoming co-producing projects include *Oedipus* (Broadway debut).

## MARÍA INÉS OLMEDO PROJECTS  Co-Producer

María Inés Olmedo is a Mexican, London-based theatre producer and maker, with over a decade of international experience across film, film festivals, theatre, and opera.

Recent credits in the West End include co-producing *A Strange Loop* (Barbican) and associate producing *Shifters* (Duke of York's), *A Mirror* (Trafalgar), and *Best of Enemies* (Noël Coward).

Projects outside the West End include producing and general managing the sold-out and four-star immersive opera production *A Fantastic Bohemian* (Arcola Theatre), which she also directed, *Invisibles* (Vault Festival), and Terrifying Women's *Gutted* (Omnibus).

Before founding María Inés Olmedo Projects in London, María Inés worked in the directing departments of leading opera companies, including Birmingham Opera Company, the Royal Opera House, and English National Opera, as well as at Playful, one of the leading producers and general managers of theatre and musicals in the West End. She began her career in Mexico City, and with over 20 critically acclaimed theatre, musical, and opera productions continues to collaborate with some of the country's most recognised artists and leading cultural institutions.

María Inés Olmedo Projects is dedicated to telling daring, vibrant, and inspiring stories across disciplines, primarily, though not exclusively, highlighting Latin American and international writers and introducing their work to wider English-speaking audiences. MIO Projects champions perspectives and voices that have a powerful universal resonance in today's world.

# Special Thanks

Matthew Byam Shaw, Helen Clarkson, Alastair Lindsey-Renton, Adam Maskell, Jack Lea, Daniel Evans, Rick Miramontez, Marie Bshara, Sam Barickman, Dana Harris, Eric Podwall, Dallas Smith, Alexandra Rae, Emma Collier, Sophie Austin, Amy Loughton, Katerina Michael, Jacob Vogelstein, Julia Brown, Jessie Newman, Drew Brody, Georgie Rankcom, Christopher & David R. Murray, Jeff Grinspoon, Jon Foley, Victoria Aguirre, Delfin Van Peborgh, Ian Tarbert, Sing Out, Louise! Productions, Yola Mezcal, Hillel Friedman, Sean Glass, Tefi Pesoa, Mark Consuelos, Marc Crousillat, Sabrina Brier, Alex Donnelly, Emilio Madrid, Zachary Hausman, Krista Smith, Tim Federle, David Lucas Shaw, Evan Cabnet, Dawn Winsor, Yale Cabaret, and Jackeline Torres.

The original Off-Broadway production of *Invasive Species* was produced by Eric Kuhn and Tre' Scott of Folk Productions, Danielle Perelman, and Adam Rodner and Ahmad Simmons of Arterial Projects. It ran from 7 May to 30 June 2024 at the Vineyard's Dimson Theatre in New York City.

The cast featured Raffaela Donatich, Alexandra Maurice, Maia Novi, and Julian Sanchez.

The creative and production teams were as follows:

| | |
|---|---|
| Director | **Michael Breslin** |
| Assistant Director | **Louisa Jacobson** |
| Dramaturg/Producer | **Amauta M. Firmino** |
| Sound Design | **Jessie Char & Maxwell Neely-Cohen** |
| Lighting Design | **Yichen Zhou** |
| Costume Design | **Cole McCarty** |
| Stage Manager | **Molly Shea** |
| Lead Producers | **Folk Productions, Danielle Perelman, Arterial Projects** |

| | |
|---|---|
| Executive Producers | **Jeremy O. Harris and Josh Godfrey** |
| Associate Producers | **David Thomas Tao and Benjamin Nelson** |
| Co-producers | **Vaughn Feighan & Chase Landow, Tira Harpaz, Brandon Sanchez, and Rachel Weiss** |
| Assistant Producer | **Sophia Englesberg** |

*Invasive Species* was originally developed at The Tank, a New York City home for emerging artists. Its developmental run began on 3 June 2023 for 14 performances only. The cast featured Raffaela Donatich, Alexandra Maurice, Maia Novi, and Julian Sanchez.

The creative and production team were as follows:

| | |
|---|---|
| Director | **Michael Breslin** |
| Assistant Director | **Louisa Jacobson** |
| Dramaturg/Producer | **Amauta M. Firmino** |
| Projections/Video Engineer | **Cameron Surh** |
| Sound Design | **Jessie Char & Maxwell Neely-Cohen** |
| Lighting Design | **Yichen Zhou** |
| Costume Design | **Cole McCarty** |
| Stage Manager | **Max Mooney** |
| Producers | **Molly FitzMaurice, Malena Grandio** |

# KING'S HEAD THEATRE

King's Head Theatre is a purpose-built, wheelchair accessible theatre with a 200-seat flexible auditorium off Upper St, Islington, which showcases a wide range of performances—from plays to musicals, opera to cabaret, and drag to comedy.

Established in 1970, King's Head Theatre was the oldest pub theatre in the UK until it closed its doors in August 2023. For 53 years, the theatre was housed in the back room of the King's Head Pub on Upper Street in an old boxing ring and pool hall, before opening the new space in Islington Square right behind the pub theatre in January 2024.

Under Artistic Director and Founder Dan Crawford, whose tenure lasted 35 years until his death in 2005, the theatre became known as a breeding ground for new talent and great work. Renowned actors like Maureen Lipman, Hugh Grant, Jennifer Saunders, Dawn French, Alan Rickman, and Richard E. Grant all performed at the theatre, and a number of productions transferred to the West End and Broadway. The venue premiered work from writers such as Steven Berkoff, Tom Stoppard, Bryony Lavery, and Victoria Wood.

In 2010, Olivier Award-winning company Opera UpClose Productions became the theatre's resident company for four years. With Adam Spreadbury-Maher as Artistic Director, they turned the King's Head into "London's Little Opera House", winning an Olivier Award for *La Boheme* in the Best New Opera category. More recently, the theatre has developed a commitment to emerging work that is daring and innovative—such as *Trainspotting*, the Edinburgh Fringe and touring immersive hit which was developed by King's Head Theatre.

The theatre showcases a lot of LGBTQ+ work which explores the full spectrum of experiences symbolised by the rainbow flag. It is a home for a new wave of theatre makers, with a focus on work which is joyful, irreverent, colourful, and queer.

In the first year of the new King's Head, the theatre has showcased work from artists such as Rob Madge, Luke Bayer, Olivier award-winner Shaun McKenna, triple Fringe First winners Xhloe & Natasha, *Heartstopper's* Cormac Hyde-Corrin, Neil Ashton, and writer Jonathan Maitland. So far in its second year, the theatre has worked with artists such as Lauren Ward, Josie Benson, Vikki Stone, Rosie Day, Jo Foster, and former artistic director Hannah Price.

# SUPPORT KING'S HEAD THEATRE

Angels of Angel Production Fund

The Angels of Angel Production Fund is a fund that is specifically used to create and produce new work in our new theatre. Your donation won't just support the creation of one production, but an ongoing range of productions. All ticket income earned from the show will be put back into the fund and used to capitalise the next one.

Support us by joining our Network of Angels or Sponsor a Stair from our 53-year history at the pub.

Find out more www.kingsheadtheatre.com

# KING'S HEAD THEATRE TEAM

| | |
|---|---|
| Executive Producer (CEO) | Sofi Berenger |
| Producer & Programmer | Zoë Weldon |
| Head of Theatre & Operations | Lily Bearwish |
| Technical Manager | Alex Lewer |
| Finance Manager | Ania Kanik |
| Marketing & Digital Producer | Katie Kirkpatrick |
| Programming & Communications Coordinator | Ailish Erskine |
| Building, Operations & Production Coordinator | Molly Hands |
| Fundraising & Development Associate | Hazel Kerr |
| Technical Supervisor | Andrea Zatvarnicka |
| Box Office Supervisor & Duty Manager | Bekah Mitchell |
| Bar Supervisor & Duty Manager | Adam Reeves |
| Ticketing & Sales Consultant | Alistair Green |
| Bookkeeper | Alan Mackintosh |
| Script Consultants | Joe von Malachowski, Matthew Greenhough |
| PR | ANR PR |

## Theatre Team Members

Alice Moloney, Atlanta Sonson-Chapman, Amelia Kirk, Andrew Swift, Bec Rolle, Bella Gervais, Charlie Lovejoy, Daniel Yazdani, Ellie Burbeary, Florence Overton, Georgie Brown, Hannah Breedon, Jahmal Swaby, James Huxtable, Jonny Iles, Maddy Whitby, Madeline Lewis, Mark Kellacher, Matilda Wilkes, Matt Heslop, Nathan Friend, Rachel Coates, Sam McHale, Sarah Morrison and Sean Leacy.

## Trustees

Rutger Beelaerts, Chris Cook, Matthew Hedges, Dawn James, Robert Khan (Chair), Kate Mullan, Aaron Porter, James Quaife, Jason Smith, and Helen Williamson.
Board Secretary: Alex Boyle

# THANKS TO OUR KING'S HEAD THEATRE SUPPORTERS

**Angels of Angel Supporters:**

Ricardo Alonso in memory of Illy Bleeding, Bert Aerts, Margie Barbour, Louise Chantal, Dugan Cummings, Tony Bonnar, Nick Perry, Kevin Elyot's Bristol Friends, Steven Felderman, Maira Boyd Hind, Matthew Hodson in memory of David Stuart, Ashley Humphreys, Sir Ben Kingsley, Dame Joanna Lumley in memory of Simon Cadell, Cameron Mackintosh, Katey Turvey, Claire Monk, Mary Rensten and Martin Court in memory of Syd Golder and the women of Greenham Common, Lois Potter, Harold Sanditen and Thanasis Kalantzis in memory of Dan Crawford, Dame Janet Suzman, John Thirlwell, Nancy Gibbs, Nicola Goldie, Tom Stoppard, Samuel Berwick, Charles Lindon, Rod Natkiel, Ashley Humphreys, Bert Aerts, Rutger Beelaerts, Maria Boyd Hind, Kiran Khetia, Martin Checov, Bernard Sharp, Adele Anderson, Gary Davy, Mark Vogel and William Denebeim.

# THANKS TO EVERYONE WHO DONATED TO OUR NEW AUDITORIUM SEATING

The Wilke Family Trust, Mark Vogel, Martin Checov, Bernard Sharp, Gary Fethke, Chris Cook, David Harding, Christine Clarke, Peter Bramah, Sam Berwick, Peter Dicks, Ricardo Alonso, William Purdy, Hamish Neave, Trixi Bücker, Bernadine Pritchett, Nicole LaFountaine, Roger Mears, Sean Mathias, Neal Foster, Maria Boyd Hind, and Kenny Wax.

# Foreword

The decision to abandon reason and devote one's life to the study of emotions—how we articulate them—is made when we are much too emotional to be trusted. I made the decision to study acting when I was 17, awkward and vulnerable, not knowing that I was signing my life away to exist in a state of awkward vulnerability for the rest of my career. That state of awkward vulnerability and the mania it inspires is baked into the inciting incident for Maia Novi's brilliant debut play *Invasive Species*, a work that, for my money, is one of the great explorations of the traumas of drama schools. Indeed, in many circles I've called it one of the great plays of the Trauma School genre.

Setting a trauma school play within a "madhouse" is inspired, but making the children trapped in the madhouse as richly empathetic as they are is moreso, because in an age of easy pleasures making children in a mental institution the joke would be such an easier sale. Yet Maia treats them each with a richness and generosity that, from her own telling, she wasn't afforded while at Yale studying acting. The madhouse being a more healing place for a young person sent there than the community they had outside of it is not in and of itself a unique idea, but it is novel when juxtaposed with the ivory tower of Yale, upper-class Argentina, and the fantasy of being Eva Perón if you just roll your Rs right.

Reading the play, I thought a lot about my first stint at drama school (I've been twice), the excitement and hope married with the constant disappointment. How absurd in all ways. How tender. How maddening. How clarifying. Maia, in her first play, did the rare thing of painting an image so clear you couldn't mistake it for anyone else's work. It was truly honest and of itself. One of the great works of the Trauma School genre.

**Jeremy O. Harris**

# INVASIVE SPECIES

## A True Story

**By Maia Novi**
**Directed and developed by Michael Breslin**
**in collaboration with Amauta M. Firmino**

The following text is the script as written before its run in London. Revisions made during the rehearsal and staging processes are not reflected in this publication. As a result, the staged production may have differed.

**Locations**

A Psych Ward, *Yesterday*

A Film Set, *Tomorrow*

A Stage, *Now*

**On Staging**

The set is purposefully plain: five stock institutional chairs and a (hopefully) clean floor. The costumes are knowingly neutral, emphasizing the idea that the five-person ensemble moves as one. Lights and sound, however, are decidedly *maximalist*. They not only inform the rapid shifts from one location to the next, they create them.

As a story about immigration and assimilation, it's no coincidence that this play primarily takes place along the slowly converging border of two vastly distinct worlds. Utilizing the logic of memory and dreams, this play shifts between the two worlds, often overlapping them as Maia, in the "here and now" of the stage struggles to keep her ground and find herself. These *shifts* should be treated with all the seamless ease of a channel flip and all the impending doom of an anxiety spiral. But above all, they should be *precise*.

**Characters**

*The play features five performers playing multiple roles.*

*Performer 1*

**Maia**, *Latina, female, 20s. An aspiring actress.*
**Evita**, *Argentinian, female, 30s. An aspiring actress.*

*Performer 2*

**Akila**, *Black, female, 16. Mischievous.*
**"Friend" A**, *younger, prettier, & more successful than you.*

*Performer 3*

**The Acting Bug**, *eternal. Thirsty.*
**Eduardo**, *latinx, 16. Never speaks.*
**Director**, *white, British? 40s. Oblivious.*
**"Friend" B**, *younger, prettier, & more successful than you.*

*Performer 4*

**Psychiatrist**, *white, 50s. Oblivious.*
**Jacob**, *latinx, 16. Rebellious.*
**Mom**, *Argentinian, 70s. Mile-a-minute, but going nowhere.*
**Dad**, *Argentinian, 70s. Terrified of anything remotely "off."*
**"Friend" C**, *younger, prettier, & more successful than you.*
**Joey**, *20s. An overworked assistant.*

*Performer 5*

**Nurse Elsa**, *white, 60s. Well-meaning, dictatorial.*
**Agent**, *white, mid-30s. If vocal fry had a face . . .*
**Blonde Bitch**, *white, 20s. It's probably meth.*
**"Friend" D**, *younger, prettier, & more successful than you.*
**Translator**. *Accurate. Too accurate?*

## On Performance & Style

This play is in part inspired by the monologues of Spalding Gray. Specifically, his 1977 production of *Rumstick Road* with the Wooster Group. In that piece, Gray and two other performers shift characters and locations on a dime. Much of this is achieved through bold staging that isn't afraid to "show the work," in other words, not hiding the "stage business." This play's frequent hops through time and space will require something similar: a willingness to suspend disbelief and let the play just be a play.

Like Gray's work, this play also aims to tame a true and traumatic story through humor. In that respect, the performance style should respect both the gravity of the situation and the humor inherent to it. While half of the play functions very much like a satire, the other half is a true story. The satire should be a send up. But the situations in this play that are based on real events and real people should be treated with respect, dignity, and compassion.

In other words, the children in this play should be taken seriously. The adults . . . not so much.

The two bilingual sections of this play introduce a Translator character who should have their own distinct personality. The characters that speak in Spanish in this play are essentially split in half between two performers and two distinct identities. This is intentional—an attempt at approximating the common experience of many polyglots who feel that they become, quite literally, another person when speaking different languages.

However, when Maia speaks Spanish, she does not have a translator. This is also intentional.

*total darkness.*
*a driving electronic beat.*
*we hear rapid, labored breaths—a struggle.*

*lights up on maia.*
*deep in a dance that we'll come to know as her "wasabi dance."*
*but that's for later. right now, she's moving—faster*
*and harder until . . .*

*blackout.*

*the ensemble members enter unseen in the darkness.*
*when the lights come up, they surround maia,*
*looking out and over the audience.*

*they're at the movies.*

*maia steps forward.*

**Maia**
The first time I watched an American movie, I felt high.
A high I've been chasing ever since.

My friends and I went to see *Spiderman*.

*The Amazing Spiderman.*

The one with Andrew Garfield and Emma Stone.

I remember walking to the screening room with my ticket in hand and being so nervous . . . like I was about to watch something exclusive, something VIP.

Like I was crossing some kind of vortex into a secret universe of infinite possibility and bright colors.

Because from the outside, everything American was so brightly colored to me. So saturated.

And for the first time, I remember watching the trailers in Spanish for the upcoming Latin-American films and feeling

like there was something inferior about them, outdated,
lame even. Like a cheap appetizer. And then . . .

> *a faint buzzing sound from offstage.*

. . . there was this weird buzzing in my ear. Like the
cheap speakers in the theater just doubled the cheapness
of everything on the screen and reminded me of all the
cheapness of living in a country that's just constantly two or
three steps behind on everything!
And how maybe that was my life? That could be my life?

> *the columbia pictures' jingle plays.*

But then . . . This BEAUTIFUL music played.

> *the ensemble exits, leaving maia alone—awed
> and in wonder.*

And this bright light came shining out of the screen . . .

> *the acting bug buzzes just offstage.*

Like the sun. Like the rising sun!
And there she was!

> *maia stretches out her hands, desperate to touch the light . . .*

The STATUE OF LIBERTY!
Inviting me. Calling me. Waiting for me.
And like a lightning strike, it hit me!

> *like a moth to the flame . . . maia collapses.
> the buzzing offstage grows in intensity until . . .*

> *enter acting bug.
> lithe and limber, a true trickster, but also a bit of a . . . thot.*

**Acting Bug**
Hi.
It's me.

I'm a bug.
But not just any bug.
I'm the *acting* bug.
These are my wings, for efficient mobility.
These are my legs, for multi-tasking.
And *this* is my proboscis for feeding.

> *he shows us how it works.*

I feed on talent.
I feed on raw talent by probing into the vein of a
young child with raw talent. The younger the better.
I look for children who want attention but don't get it.
Children whose parents ignore them.
Kids who love to lie.
Kids who like to be looked at.
Kids who need the world to revolve around them.
Little FREAKS!! Like her . . .

> *a spotlight on maia, still catatonic on the floor.*
> *he lifts her up like a piece of raw meat.*

You see that thing in her eyes?
That desperation?
That's what I'm looking for.

> *he straddles her.*

I stick my proboscis into their necks and I spit a little.

> *he spits on her face.*
> *a thick glob of spit.*

Because I don't have a stomach!
I don't have a stomach so I have to digest before I eat.

> *he flips her over and . . .*

So I drop some spit into my proboscis
And it mixes with the blood, which is where
talent lives and then I . . .

*he stretches her body into an unnatural shape.*
*this <u>looks</u> <u>painful</u> and violent.*

Suck. It. Up.

*but maia doesn't react. she stares out calmly.*

And what gets left behind is a bit of my spit.
Which produces a kind of allergy in the host.
And the allergy is an illness, that goes creeping into their brains
And seeping into their bodies
Until it finally manifests as an insane desire to be a professional actor!

*the bug stands maia up on her feet, like a puppet.*

And it happens like this . . .

*the acting bug sucks on maia's neck then . . .*
*pushes her into a spotlight.*

**Maia**
I left my home.
I left my friends and family.
I even left myself.
No matter what it took
I was going to be in the American movies.

My name is Maia.
This is a true story.

*lights shift a*
*driving electronic beat.*

**Maia**
Step one: Get out of Argentina.

I had always acted out, but I had never acted.
I fled to France first, where I studied acting with a group of sweaty sad clowns all dressed in black who promised me something called a "certificate in acting."

That sounded like a good place to start.

> *the ensemble becomes a troupe of french clowns.*
> *their poses are intentional, profound, prepared.*

**French Clown**
You could be a star in Europe!

**Another French Clown**
Stay with us!

**Maia**
But in Europe they make sad films about tiny people,
while in America they make Superhero movies and
TV shows with seasons that last longer than most
South American governments.
And besides . . .
I didn't even speak French.

**French Clown**
We don't care!

**Maia**
I was aiming higher.
They didn't understand the high that I was after.

> *maia pushes the clowns away, dispelling them.*

**Maia**
Step two: get out of France.

If I wanted to be in the real movies, I needed to get into a
real drama school. So I googled—"best drama schools in the
world" and took the first train to London.

**Ensemble**
How's your RP?

**Maia**
My what?

**Ensemble**
Your "received pronunciation."

**Maia**
Oh I received it from my mother, she talks a lot.
You'll see.

**Ensemble**
No. No. Your British accent.

**Maia**
Oh! It's *fabulous*. It's *fantastic!* And *I love the pub!*

*the ensemble turns their backs on her.*

**Maia**
I could already tell this wasn't going to work.
I had to aim higher.
I had to shoot for the top!
I had to move to the center of it all!
I had to go to NEW . . .

*a drum roll.*

**Maia**
. . . Haven . . . ?

*the ensemble become teachers.*

**Maia**
Apparently Yale had a drama school, and there was a direct pipeline from their classrooms into the American movies. That sounded like the place for me.
So I prepared a monologue. But I was so nervous, I completely blacked out.

So I made something up.

*maia improvises a couple of lines from her "monologue,"*
*something along the lines of:*

**Maia**
*Yes, I cheated on you,*
*And no, I don't feel bad,*
*I loved it!*

*For the first time in years,*
*I felt something,*
*In my, UGHHH*

> *maia grunts.*

*Oh you're crying now?*
*Baby, you had your chance,*
*You had my heart and you could've done whatever you wanted with it*
*But instead you chewed on it, like a sneakers,*
*Like a candy bar!*

> *silence.*
> *somewhere between stunned and . . . awkward.*

**Teachers**
Where's that monologue from?

**Teacher**
It's from *Spiderman*?
*The Amazing Spiderman*?
The one with Andrew Garfield and Emma Stone,
But adapted into Spanish,
And then re-translated into English.

**Teachers**
Oooh. We love your accent!

**Maia**
They wanted me!
It was obvious.
But a month into the program . . .

**Teachers**
Hm . . . that doesn't quite sound right.

**Maia**
And a year into the program . . .

**Teachers**
Can you do it more American?

**Maia**
But I thought you loved my accent!

**Teacher One**
You have a lazy tongue.
And you move your hands too much.

**Teacher Two**
They get in the way of your truth.

> *an ensemble member ties maia's hands up.*

**Maia**
And three years into the program . . .

**Teacher One**
The accent, it's still sort of . . .

**Teacher Two**
Unplaceable.

**Teacher Three**
Unmarketable.

**Teacher Four**
UnAmerican.

**Teacher One**
But imitation might work!

**Teacher Two**
Just . . . pick a celebrity!

**Teacher Three**
Someone you wanna be like,

**Maia**
Uhm . . .

**Teachers**
What about someone like:

> *gwyneth paltrow's amplified voice interrupts the scene with . . .*

**Gwyneth Paltrow**
*"Good morning guys I'm gonna take you through my morning goop routine."*

**Maia**
Step three . . . sound like Gwyneth Paltrow.

> *maia repeats after gwyneth, doing her best to sound like her.*

**Maia**
*"Good morning guys I'm gonna take you through my morning goop routine."*

They told me to repeat that phrase as a workout for my tongue muscles.

I had to say that one particular phrase in this one particular way, until I couldn't even remember the sound of my own voice.

That key phrase became my mantra.
Every day. Non stop. Playing in my head.
At the gym.
In the shower.
At the cafe with the stale bagels and the warm cream cheese.

*"Good morning guys I'm gonna take you through my morning goop routine."*

And the clock was ticking.
My showcase was coming up.
Every actor does a showcase before they graduate from a drama program. For most students, it's like . . . somewhere between a field trip, a job interview, and . . . legalized human trafficking.

Showcase looms over the entire school like a dark cloud.

**Ensemble One**
It's your debut.

**Ensemble Two**
Your one shot.

14  Invasive Species

**Ensemble Three**
The most important day of your life.

**Maia**
But for me, it was my one shot at getting an artist VISA. My ticket to staying in the USA.
I needed to book an agent. I needed to book a job. I needed attention and I needed it fast.
Because no showcase, no visa
No visa, no movies
And no movies, back to the cheap speakers . . .
And the shitty movie theaters and . . .
And I . . . and I . . .

*maia dispels an intrusive thought.*

**Maia**
No!
I was going to be in the American movies!

*the ensemble moves as one.*

**Ensemble**
If you're going to work in this industry, then you need to sound like Gwyneth!

**Maia**
And so I pushed harder! I fell deeper. Watching videos of Gwyneth on repeat. Interviews. Podcasts. Movies.

**Ensemble**
Everything Gwyneth Eats In a Day.

**Maia**
"I usually have a glass or two of water . . . "

**Ensemble**
Gwyneth Paltrow Cooks Her Breakfast Frittata!

**Maia**
"I actually think it's a strong feminist statement to cook for the people you love."

**Ensemble**
Smoothie Queens Gwyneth and Hailey Bieber Play A Game of Smell.

**Maia**
"Hailey, what if I told you I fucked your dad
in the bathroom?"

> *the ensemble laughs like gwyneth.*

**Maia**
One week later I started to experience horrible insomnia. Deep down I knew I had to give Gwyneth a break. But the tongue is a muscle!

**Ensemble**
Use it or lose it bitch!
Gwyneth Paltrow on Spanish and Cooking.

**Maia**
*"Por supuesto!* I speak Spanish and I speak uhm, enough French to, you know, do interviews and—"

**Ensemble**
Gwyneth Paltrow Dishes On Wellness Treatments, Beauty Tips, And More.

**Maia**
"I usually take a bath with baking soda and salt because a naturopath once told me that, like, helps pull the radiation out . . . that you get in the sky."

**Ensemble**
Gwyneth Paltrow On Her Blended Family & Raising Teens.

**Maia**
"You know I really believe that life, especially for women, comes in chapters."

**Ensemble**
Gwyneth Paltrow Reflects on Her Relationship with Weinstein and the Aftermath.

**Maia**
"I just hope I'm drinking Bill Gates's water."

**Ensemble**
Inside Gwyneth's Paltrow's 90s Fashion Archive.

**Maia**
"I wore this when I was going out with Brad Pitt / at some premiere—"

**Ensemble**
/Get Hamptons Ready with Gwyneth Paltrow.

**Maia**
"I don't usually read / things about myself—"

**Ensemble**
Gwyneth Paltrow Wins Best Actress.

**Ensemble**
Wins best actress.

**Ensemble**
Wins best actress.

**Ensemble**
Wins best actress . . .

*maia bangs her head against the floor.*

**Maia**
I tried melatonin, valerian, CBD, light therapy, masturbation, you name it. Gwyneth haunted my dreams. So I made an appointment with a psychiatrist. March 15th, 2022. I was 25 years old.

*enter psychiatrist and nurse elsa.*

**Maia**
You know, it's really hard to explain what's going on in your head in any language but even harder in a language like English.
English is like . . .

*maia gestures "english".*

**Maia**
But I grew up speaking . . .

*maia gestures "spanish".*

**Maia**
You know what I mean?

**Psychiatrist**
No.
Are your thoughts always this disorganized?

**Maia**
What?

*over-articulating.*

**Psychiatrist**
Do you struggle to articulate?

**Maia**
You know what?
Don't worry about it.
I'm just gonna go now . . .

*maia starts to walk away.*

**Psychiatrist**
I'm afraid you can't do that.

*a nurse emerges.*

See if this helps. You can stay here the night, and if it works, we'll send you home tomorrow with a prescription.

*the nurse stretches out her hand.*

**Psychiatrist**
Rest will be good for you.

*maia hesitates then walks slowly towards the nurse.
she looks at the pill, then at the audience.*

## Maia
I needed sleep.
And they told me I'd only be one night.
Right?

> *maia takes the pill.*
>
> *lights shift.*
>
> *we're in the common room of a youth psychiatric ward.*
> *akila sits on a couch, staring out to the audience, deadpan.*
> *jacob paces, tracing the perimeter of the stage,*
> *deep in thought about something.*
> *eduardo off to the side, staring out at the audience.*
> *and maia hides behind a column . . . eavesdropping . . .*

## Jacob
Psst! Can I . . . uh—
*Play Roblox on your phone . . . ?*

## Akila
Shhh!!

> *akila looks over her shoulder, making sure nobody heard that.*

## Akila
Are you serious? Shut up.

## Jacob
Please . . . just 10 minutes?

## Akila
No.

## Jacob
I'll give you a jello?

> *akila considers this.*
> *she shakes her head—no deal.*

## Jacob
OK. Three?

**Akila**
Two now. Two tomorrow.

> *it's a deal.*
> *jacob makes sure no one is watching.*
> *he slides her a jello snack pack.*
> *akila slips it in her pocket.*

**Akila**
8pm in my room.

**Jacob**
7pm.

**Akila**
7pm is TV time. I'm not missing TV time.

**Maia**
Hi . . .

> *maia steps out from behind the column.*
> *jacob and akila eye her suspiciously . . .*
> *scanning her from head to toe.*
> *eduardo doesn't, he just stares out at the audience, deadpan.*
> *silence.*

**Maia**
Do you guys know . . . if there's a phone I can use?
Or like . . . where they put my stuff? I can't find my phone.

> *the kids look at her like she's some strange specimen.*

**Jacob**
Why are you so old?

**Maia**
Uh . . .

**Jacob**
And you sound weird.
Why do you sound so weird?

**Akila**
You look rich.
How tall are you?

**Maia**
I'm one meter seventy-five centimeters.

> *akila and jacob giggle.*

**Akila and Jacob**
What!?

**Jacob**
You're so weird . . .

> *they chuckle.*

**Maia**
What is this place?

**Jacob**
What do you think?

**Maia**
Some kind of . . . children's hospital?

**Jacob**
Not exactly.

**Maia**
A jail?

**Jacob**
Almost.

**Maia**
Am I dead?

**Akila**
You wish.

> *lights shift.*

**Maia**
There were playing cards, puzzles, there were children's books and there was a TV.
The last thing I remember is they gave me a sleeping pill.
Did they transport me in my sleep?
Where are my clothes?
Why are there no adults here?
There are no windows and there are bars on the doors.
Am I in a—
*(back to the kids)*
Psychiatric hospital?

**Jacob**
Bingo.

**Maia**
*(aside)*
But it wasn't just any psychiatric hospital.
It was a psychiatric hospital for children.
A youth ward.
They put me in the Youth Ward.
The oldest kid was sixteen. The youngest . . . maybe 12.
Why did they put me here?
I had to wait for a "doctor" to explain it to me, apparently.
In the meantime all I could do was wait and write.
Take note of everything I saw, everything I heard.
And when I wasn't writing I was reading Caryl Churchill, the only thing they let me keep.

> *maia pulls out caryl churchill's complete works.*

Her photo was on the cover.
This kid Jacob asked:

**Jacob**
"Is that Einstein?"

**Maia**
Jacob is 15, and seems angry all the time.
He has a friend Eduardo, who's 13, and never speaks.

Then there's Akila. She's 16. She's the boss here.
There were others but this trio were the only ones that stuck together.
They called themselves "The suicide squad"
A few days after I got there Akila came to me.
I was sitting in a chair staring at the clock.
And she just walked over . . .

*akila walks over.*

Said nothing.
And just dropped a Jello on my lap.

*akila drops a jello and walks away.*

**Maia**
That's when I realized that Jello is like currency here.
And that maybe . . . she liked me?

*enter nurse elsa.*

**Nurse Elsa**
Maia!
Med time!

*she jabs a cup of medication at maia.*

**Maia**
What is this?

**Nurse Elsa**
Just take it.

**Maia**
I need to know what it is before I take it.

**Nurse Elsa**
Doctor's orders. Not mine.

**Maia**
But / what kind—

**Nurse Elsa**
Look, either you take it or . . .
I'll have to report it to the / doctors.

**Akila**
/ Just fucking take it.

**Nurse Elsa**
Language!

**Jacob**
If you don't it's worse! Just take it!

**Nurse Elsa**
1 . . . 2 . . . .

**Maia**
WASABI!

*maia slaps the air in front of her.*

*(aside)*
That was a word I would say to myself whenever I had an intrusive thought or emotion.
WASABI!

*maia takes her pills.*

*time passes.*

*maia approaches the kids.*

**Maia**
So . . . how long have you been here?

**Jacob**
All her life.

**Akila**
Ooooohhh! Shut up!

**Jacob**
It's true.
12 times.

**Akila**
Shut. Up.
(*to Maia*)
His dad is a Republican.

**Jacob**
So?!

**Akila**
Eduardo's too.

*eduardo doesn't react.*

**Maia**
I'm sorry.
I guess?

**Akila**
What's your name?

**Maia**
Maia. With an I.

**Akila**
Is that a Russian name?

**Maia**
Yeah actually!

**Akila**
Is it true that in Russia people eat cats?

**Maia**
Uh . . . I wouldn't know actually. I'm not—

**Akila**
Are you a model?

**Maia**
Haha. No.
I'm an actress.

**Akila**
Like TikTok?

**Maia**
No, just like a regular actor.
Studying to . . . you know, hopefully be in the movies one day.

**Akila**
So you haven't been in a movie?

**Maia**
Not yet.

**Akila**
Then you're not a real actor.

**Maia**
Yes I am.

**Akila**
Anyone can say "I'm an actor" if they haven't been in anything.

**Maia**
I—I—No I'm like actually . . .
I'm *studying* acting. I'm an actor.

**Akila**
Prove it then.

**Maia**
What?

**Akila**
I said. Prove it!

> *lights shift.*
>
> *enter acting bug with a ring light.*
>
> *and ensemble member with a photo backdrop.*
>
> *maia films a self-tape audition.*

**Reader**
"Evita Duarte! It's over! You're fired."

**Maia**
"I won't do it again, I promise."

**Reader**
*(With a lot of emotion)*
"First you interrupt my interrogation, Then you take his side
And then you . . . follow him to his house and *sleep* with him?"

> *maia struggles to find the next line.*

**Maia**
Uhh . . . OK. Stop. Sorry. Could you just . . .
That was a bit too much. Like it threw me off.

**Reader**
What do you mean?

**Maia**
Like can you do less . . . character.

**Reader**
So you don't want me to help you, acting wise?

**Maia**
No, I mean, it's just a self tape? So can you just cue me?

**Reader**
OK. OK. Whatever you say. Ready?

**Maia**
Yes.

**Reader**
*(lifeless)*
"Evita Duarte. It's over. You're fired."

**Maia**
"I won't do it again. I promise!"

**Reader**
*(even more lifeless)*
"First you interrupt my interrogation,
then you take his side and—"

**Maia**
OK no I mean, you can help me a little bit, but just like don't play a character.

**Reader**
OK. I also need to leave in like 20 minutes just so you know.

**Maia**
No problem.
Let's do it!

**Reader**
"Evita Duarte, it's over. You're fired."

**Maia**
"I won't do it again, I promise!"

**Reader**
"First you interrupt my interrogation, then you take his side and then you follow him to his house and sleep with him?"

**Maia**
"I did not take his side."

**Reader**
"You think I'm stupid?"

**Maia**
"At least one of us was trying to make it happen."

**Reader**
"By getting in bed with a sleazebag . . ."

**Maia**
"He's not a sleez-bug."

**Reader**
Uh—wait. Let's start over.

**Maia**
What? Why'd you stop? That was a good take!

**Reader**
It's just . . .
It's pronounced SleaZZZ-baaag.

**Maia**
What?

**Reader**
SleaZZZ-baaag/

**Maia**
Sleez-bug?

**Reader**
SLEAZ—BAG

**Maia**
SLEEZBUG!

> *the acting bug emerges from behind the backdrop.*

**Reader**
Bag! Not bug! It's a slight sound shift. (*Nasal*) *AAAAA. Not AAAHHHH.*

**Maia**
I get it.

**Reader**
OK. Let's go!

**Reader**
"Evita Duarte. It's over. You're fired!"

**Maia**
"I won't do it again I promise!"

**Reader**
"First you interrupt my interrogation, then you take his side and then you . . . follow him to his house and sleep with him?"

**Maia**
"I did not take his side."

**Reader**
"You think I'm stupid?"

**Maia**
"At least one of us was trying to make it happen."

**Reader**
"By getting in bed with a sleaze bag?"

**Maia**
"He's not A SLEEZEBAAAAAAAAAG!!!"

> *maia thrashes the backdrop against the floor.*
>
> *the ensemble backs away, until maia exhausts herself and . . .*
> *lights shift.*
> *a dark stage.*
> *a single spotlight on maia.*
>
> *enter psychiatrist and director from opposite sides.*
>
> *they slowly walk out of the shadows, encroaching on maia at the center.*

**Psychiatrist**
Maia?

**Director**
Maia?

**Maia**
Yes.

**Director**
I loved your tape . . .

**Psychiatrist**
So I heard . . . you didn't want to take your medication?

**Maia**
I just don't know what it is.

**Director**
I *loved* your tape.

**Maia**
Thanks!

**Psychiatrist**
Let's talk about how you got that bruise on your forehead . . .

**Maia**
What bruise?

**Director**
*The* Bruce! Bruce Springsteen?
We're considering him for the role of your husband.

**Maia**
Oh!

**Psychiatrist**
You need to be able to trust us if we're gonna work though your symptoms.

**Director**
I'm ready whenever you are.

**Maia**
Should I start with the monologue?

**Psychiatrist**
An inner monologue?

**Director**
Yes, contemporary, under 2 minutes.

**Psychiatrist**
Is it your own voice?

**Maia**
Yes, this is my natural accent.

**Director**
OK keep going.

**Maia**
I just can't make it stop.

**Psychiatrist**
Any family history of mental illness?

**Maia**
Hm . . . Does Chekhov count?

**Psychiatrist**
So schizophrenia. You know that's inherited . . . ?

**Director**
Anything newer?

**Maia**
I've been asking for a few days now to use a phone?

**Psychiatrist**
What about recreational drugs?

**Maia**
What?! No! Never.

**Director**
That's great.

**Psychiatrist**
Have you ever seen a psychiatrist for this before?

**Maia**
No . . .

**Director**
By the way, can you sing?
There's this song, I don't know if you know it—

**Maia**
Please, this is all a misunderstanding!
I just wanted—

**Director**
. . . '80s pop rock?

**Psychiatrist**
It's the only way to—

**Director**
Make a huge biopic!

**Psychiatrist**
To stabilize you—

**Director**
An emotionally riveting—

**Psychiatrist**
Treatment plan—

**Director**
An awards magnet—

**Psychiatrist**
And if you don't cooperate . . .

**Maia**
I'd be happy to tape again.

**Director**
We'd love you to—

**Maia**
It's one of my favourite songs.

**Psychiatrist**
There's nothing I can do about that.

**Maia**
But how long will I be—

**Psychiatrist**
That all depends on you.

**Director**
A martyr who—

**Maia**
You said I could call—

**Director**
The one and only—
Evita.
Evita PERÓN.

> *lights shift.*
>
> *we're at the ward.*
>
> *enter nurse elsa, with a cell phone in hand.*
>
> *akila chasing close behind her.*

**Nurse Elsa**
We've been over this a million times.
You should've turned it in when you arrived.

**Akila**
Just don't tell my mom.

**Nurse Elsa**
You'll just have to tell her yourself.

> *nurse elsa walks off.*

**Jacob**
There goes Roblox . . .
What are we supposed to do now?

> *akila sits down, frustrated.*

**Maia**
Was that a phone? Do you have a phone?

**Jacob**
Not anymore . . .

**Akila**
Shut up.

> *silence.*

**Maia**
How did you get it in here?

> *silence. the teens walk away.*

**Maia**
Who's Roblox?

**Jacob**
What?
Are you retarded?

**Akila**
It's a phone game.

**Maia**
Oh, like snake?

**Akila**
No.

**Jacob**
You. Are. SO old.
It's actually disturbing.
Why did they put you here?!
Actually I don't even wanna know.

*beat.*

**Maia**
I don't know.
One moment I was asking for a sleeping pill . . .
And then suddenly I was here.
Now they won't even let me check my phone for—

*silence.*

**Jacob**
OK chill.
I wasn't actually asking.
I don't care.

*beat.*

**Maia**
It's not like I wanna be here anyways.
There's been some kind of mistake.
I'm not supposed to be here.

**Jacob**
That's what I'm saying.

**Akila**
What makes you say that?

**Jacob**
Because she's like 50 years old!

**Akila**
No, I'm asking *her*.
What makes you think you don't belong here?

**Maia**
Because I'm not . . .

*maia's on the spot.*

**Akila**
Not what?

**Maia**
I'm not cra . . . supposed to be in a psych ward.
I didn't ask to be here.

**Akila**
Neither did we.
Did you ask to be here Jacob?

**Jacob**
Nope.

*akila corners maia.*

**Akila**
You think you're better than us?

**Maia**
I didn't say that.

**Jacob**
I can see it on your face.

**Akila**
You must be here for a reason.
Why are you really here?

36     Invasive Species

> *maia is cornered, she deflects.*

**Maia**
Look, I just need to get out of here.
He said you've been here 12 times.
So you must know how to get out of here.

**Akila**
What makes you think I would tell you?
I don't even know you yet.

**Nurse Elsa**
Maia. You get one phone call today.
Akila . . . you don't get anything.

> *akila sucks her teeth.*

**Maia**
Really?
Now?

**Nurse Elsa**
Ten minutes.

> *lights shift.*
>
> *maia stares at the phone in her hand.*

**Maia**
I wasted the first five minutes trying to remember a phone number. Any phone number.
But the only ones I could think of were 911 and . . .
My mom.

> *ring. ring.*
>
> *enter mom, a glamorous woman.*
> *and translator, trying their best.*

**Mom**
MAIUCHAAAA MI AMOOOOORRRRRRR
COMO ESTAS?!

**Translator**
Maiucha. My love. How are you?

**Maia**
Bien. Eh . . . estas ocupada?
*(good, uh, are you busy?)*

**Mom**
Que te esta pasando?
Lo puedo sentir, algo te esta pasando.

**Translator**
What's going on?
I can feel something's off.

**Maia**
No. No . . . Solo queria hablar.
*(No. No . . . I just wanted to talk.)*

**Mom**
Necesitas plata? Cuánto necesitas?
No me gusta hablar de plata, dame un numero.

**Translator**
Do you need money? How much do you need?
I don't like to talk about money, just give me a number.

**Maia**
No. No es plata.
*(No. It's not money.)*

**Mom**
Si estas triste, hacé como SEX AT THE CITY y andá a Balthazars.

**Translator**
If you're sad, do like SEX AT THE CITY and go to Balthazars.

**Maia**
No estoy en New York . . . Estoy en New Haven.
*(I'm not in New York . . . I'm in New Haven.)*

38   Invasive Species

**Mom**
Con tu papa ibamos todo el tiempo antes que se casara con esa mujer . . .

**Translator**
With your dad we would go all the time before he married that woman.

**Mom**
No puedo creer que eligiste vivr con el y no conmigo.

**Translator**
I can't believe you picked him instead of me.

**Maia**
Escuchá—estoy en—
encerrada en un—
*(Listen—I'm . . . I'm . . . locked up in a . . . )*

> *maia stutters.*

**Mom**
Encerrada? Como?!

**Translator**
Locked up?! How's that?!

**Mom**
Tenés que salir! El campo te hace bien!

**Translator**
You've got to get out! The outdoors are healthy.

> *maia hesitates.*

**Maia**
No, ma. Escuchá—
*(No mom. Listen—)*

**Mom**
Yo stoy en el campo de Mare disfrutando. NO SABES LO QUE ERA EL CHEESECAKE QUE HABIA AYER.

**Translator**
I'm in the country with Mare. YOU WOULDN'T BELIEVE THE CHEESECAKE I HAD LAST NIGHT.

**Mom**
Me sentí super top, super New Yorker.

**Translator**
I felt super "top", super New Yorker.

**Mom**
Después no como nada el resto de la semana.

**Translator**
Then I'll starve myself the rest of the week.

**Mom**
Y vos estas comiendo Maia?
Maia?

**Translator**
And you Maia, are you eating? . . .

**Mom / Translator**
Maia?

**Maia**
Estoy en un hospital psiquiatrico!
*(I'm in a Psychiatric Hospital)*

**Mom**
Ahora?

**Translator**
Right now?

**Maia**
Si.

**Mom**
Puah! Y por eso estas triste. A mi me metieron en uno tambien. Si pensas que lo estas pasando mal, yo lo pase peor.

**Translator**
Puah! So that's why you're sad. They put me in one too.
You think you've got it bad, I've had it worse.

*lights glitch between worlds.*

*we're back at the ward.*

*click.*

**Nurse**
Maia! Time's up.

**Maia**
I didn't even get five minutes—

*nurse elsa takes the phone out of maia's hands/*

**Nurse Elsa**
Next time.

**Maia**
Wait—wait! Can I just have a minute more?

*silence.*

*nurse elsa stares her down.*

**Maia**
I need to talk to the president!
Of Yale!

*nurse elsa "takes note" and exits.*
*maia yells after her.*

**Maia**
Please! Please! This is illegal!
I have to do my—I'm gonna miss my showcase!
Please!

**Akila**
Oh boy . . .

**Jacob**
(*to Akila*)
I told you.

> *maia slumps to the floor.*

**Akila**
Listen, you can't say shit like that.
Like you want to meet the president.

**Maia**
I didn't.

**Akila**
This isn't Russia, OK?

**Maia**
No, I'm not even—
This is all a misunderstanding.
Nobody knows I'm here like . . .

**Jacob**
You sound manic. Are you manic?

**Maia**
No. I'm just worried that no one on the outside knows where I am, so . . . they won't know how to get me out of here.

**Akila**
Uh . . . That's not how it works.

**Maia**
How does it work then?

**Akila**
I'll tell you . . . If you tell me why you're *really* here.

**Maia**
I already told you. I don't know.

**Akila**
What about that bruise on your head?

**Maia**
What?! No. Wait—

**Akila**
Denial.

**Maia**
How often do you get phone calls?

**Jacob**
Delusions. Personality disorder?

**Maia**
I couldn't even ask for help!

**Akila**
Maybe . . .

**Maia**
People will think I'm dead!

**Akila**
She definitely sounds manic.

**Maia**
No. I'm just an actor!
I have a big personality. This is how I talk.

**Akila**
Big personality . . .

> *blank stares. they shake their heads.*

**Maia**
Actors are big! We've got big personalities!
That's what we do.
Like the actors in the movies!
Do you guys not watch movies?

**Jacob**
Too long.

**Akila**
Didn't you love *Encanto*?

**Jacob**
Shut up . . . I just liked that one song.

**Maia**
Bruno?
*(she sings)*
We don't talk about Brunooo.

**Jacob**
Eww! Ew.

**Maia**
*(she sings)*
Nooo, nooo, nooo

> *jacob hides his eyes.*
> *akila smiles. she's into it.*
> *eduardo perks up.*

**Akila**
You can kind of sing.

**Maia**
See! That's because I'm a real actor.

**Jacob**
I think they're giving her uppers.

**Akila**
How do you become an actor anyways?

**Maia**
That's a great question actually.
I guess it starts with wanting to become a different person.
And then you start thinking like a different person,
Until you and that other person merge into one.

**Akila**
Ooh, so *that's* why you're here.

**Maia**
Wait, you guys, the Oscars are coming up! We should watch them!

**Jacob**
You act crazy.
You know that, right?

**Maia**
That's just how I am!

**Akila**
Do you think you're crazy?

**Maia**
... Me?

*lights shift.*

**Maia**
People have called me that before,
Like the night I entered the youth ward,
I wasn't sleeping,
And the CBD wasn't hitting.
So I went on a date.

*spanish guitars play in the background.*

*we're at a cheap mexican restaurant.*

*enter doug, a bro.*

**Doug**
Maia?

**Maia**
Doug? Am I saying it right?

**Doug**
Yeah. I like how you say it.
You ever been here?

**Maia**
No ...

*maia and doug sit at a table.*

**Doug**
The tacos here really slap.

I got a vibe from your profile that you would be into it.
*Argentina* right?

**Maia**
Uhhhhh yeah! Argentina.

**Doug**
Wow . . .

**Maia**
I know.

**Doug**
I've never been to South America but my grandparents are like immigrants? So I've always felt really connected. Maybe that's why I liked you.

**Maia**
Where is your family from?

**Doug**
Like Irish.

**Maia**
. . .

**Doug**
So do you have a *type*?
What's your type?

**Maia**
Uh. I like people that can make me laugh.
If you can't make me laugh, it's not going to work out.

> *doug laughs a bit too loud.*

**Doug**
OK! OK!
I can be funny. I can be funny.

**Maia**
Do *you* have a type?

**Doug**
Oh yeah definitely.
Blonde women just don't do it for me.

**Maia**
Right.
But.
That's not a type. That's like, the opposite of a type.

**Doug**
You sure you don't want anything?
The tacos here really slap.

**Maia**
No. I don't really like Mexican food.

**Doug**
You don't like Mexican food?!

**Maia**
No. Why? Is that weird?

**Doug**
Nah, it's not. Just be yourself.
So . . . tell me about you.
What do you do?
Do you miss home?

**Maia**
I do. But I'm an actress.
It's hard to make a living from acting back there.

**Doug**
Right, like crime and drugs and stuff?
Pablo Escobar type shit?

*the spanish guitars freeze.*

*maia turns to the audience.*

**Maia**
He was so American he thought the world started in Canada and ended in Cancún. I could say anything to him and he would believe it.

*(to doug)*
Yeah! The narcos are everywhere but the cocaine is great. We even use it as sweetener.

>*the spanish guitars return.*

**Doug**
Oh right, I know. I read about that on Vice.

**Maia**
Yeah . . .

**Doug**
Is your family staying safe?

**Maia**
Psssh! Safe? My family is *dangerous*.

**Doug**
Oh shit! Are they super bad-ass? Like . . . street smart?

**Maia**
Yeah. Especially my *abuelitas*.

**Doug**
What do you mean?!

**Maia**
I don't wanna scare you.

**Doug**
No please, tell me.

>*a trill on the guitars.*
>*a dramatic spotlight on maia's face.*
>
>*she suddenly leaps up out of her seat.*
>
>*maia begins a dance.*

**Maia**
I was born in "La Capital de Buenos Aires," a block away from the largest *tortilla* factory in the world. My abuelita Silvia used to cut *crack* in the tortilla ovens, and that's how she got her nickname, *Tortillita Loca*.

**Doug**
Oh shit!

**Maia**
My other abuela . . . Amy / she was—

**Doug**
/ Amy?!

**Maia**
I mean "Amelia." She was the *jefa* of a crew of drug runners on a river called El Dorado. She had magic in her hands. She could cook any dish: *arepas, patacones, tacos al pastor, paella, pan de yuca,* you name it!

**Doug**
Wait but that's Mexican food . . . I thought you didn't like—

**Maia**
No! Let me finish. She taught me her secrets. So by the time I was seven, I had the magic in my hands too!

**Doug**
What are you saying? It doesn't make any sense.

**Maia**
Let me finish! I could cook any dish: Arepas / patacones—

**Doug**
You're lying to me!

**Maia**
Just let me finish! Arepas, patacones /

**Doug**
What's wrong with you?!
You're crazy!

*doug exits.*

*lights shift.*

*total darkness.*

*maia on stage alone in a spotlight.*

**Maia**
Hi, my name is Maia.
And I'll be reading for the role of Eva Perón.
(she sings "Don't Cry For Me Argentina" then . . . )
I'm 5.10.
Thanks so much for giving me the opportunity to tape again.

*(she continues singing until . . . )*

DON'T CRY!!!

*lights shift suddenly.*

*we're back at the ward.*

*the kids sit in a wide semi-circle as nurse elsa leads a group therapy session.*

**Nurse Elsa**
Thank you . . . Maia . . . For that . . . offering.
Anyone else?
What about you Jacob?

**Jacob**
What about me?

**Nurse Elsa**
A daily goal and an offering.

**Jacob**
Yeah. My goal is to get discharged and my
offering is . . . Um . . . No, umm . . . My offering is
that . . . Eduardo I like your shirt.

*eduardo smiles.*

**Nurse Elsa**
There we go Eduardo!
Look at you!

*eduardo immediately goes deadpan again.*

**Nurse Elsa**
Oh come on Eduardo. We love to see you smile!
How about . . . you give Jacob a big hug in exchange for his lovely offering?

> *eduardo stares at elsa.*
> *jacob sucks his teeth.*

**Jacob**
Why are you talking to him like a baby?

**Nurse Elsa**
Jacob, don't start.

**Jacob**
He's a grown ass kid who just doesn't want to talk right now.
It's not like he's—
I don't know. It's not like he's a baby or like retarded—

**Nurse Elsa**
We don't use that word here, Jacob!

**Akila**
Here we go again . . .

**Jacob**
I'm just being honest.
No one else is!

**Nurse Elsa**
OK, thank you for sharing, Jacob.
If we're being honest, then you know perfectly well that you already *have* been discharged. But we can't let you out if no one comes to pick you up.

**Jacob**
I gave you his number.

**Nurse Elsa**
That wasn't your dad, Jacob, and we both know it.
We need a legal guardian to come pick you up.

> *jacob rubs his face in frustration.*

**Nurse Elsa**
OK let's put a pin in that.
Akila? Goal and offering?

**Akila**
Yeah, my goal is . . . watching the Oscars.

**Nurse Elsa**
Oh . . . I didn't know you liked movies Akila.

**Akila**
Yeah. Maia told me all about it.
The Oscars are good for like the imagination and stuff.

**Maia**
She's right.

**Nurse Elsa**
Well resting is our top priority here, and they're after our bedtime.
Besides, not everyone loves the Oscars as much as you . . . Maia.

**Akila**
But all we ever watch is sports and like . . . the news!
Which is boring.
Who wants to watch the Oscars, raise your hand?

*maia and jacob raise their hands first.*

*then akila looks to eduardo.*
*he raises his hand.*

**Akila**
See? Everybody loves the Oscars.

*lights shift.*

*eduardo suddenly pulls a baseball cap out of his pocket and becomes . . . .*
*the director, prepping maia for a camera test.*

*maia turns.*

**Director**
Look down.

*maia looks down.*

**Director**
Look up.

*maia looks up.*

**Director**
Smile.

*maia smiles.*

**Director**
Wider.

*maia smiles wider.*

**Director**
Fantastic. OK.
You look great.

**Maia**
Oh, thanks!

**Director**
Listen, to be candid here, we pinned two other girls for this,
Big names. But I'm really pushing for you. OK?
Oh! Here they come! Here they come! The EXECS.

*the ensemble become "film execs".*

**Director**
Take a seat guys, take a seat.
Get up on the chair.
This is Maia, she's from Argentina. The real deal!
Big fan of this script, right?

**Maia**
Oh yeah. Love it . . .

**Director**
So this is an exercise I learned from Sir Ridley.

Ridley fucking Scott!
Anyways just keep up.
Alright?

> *the "execs" get ready to take note.*
> *maia stands up on a chair.*

**Director**
I want you to go back, to your childhood.

**Maia**
Mine or Evita's?

**Director**
What? The—the—There is NO DIFFERENCE!
Is there?

> *he winks an eye at the execs, laughs.*

**Maia**
Uh, no, NO!

**Director**
Exactly . . .

> *lights shift, taking on a nefarious feel.*

**Director**
You're 7 years old.
*It's 1926 . . . or 2006, I don't know.*
And you're in a shack in the Argentinean pampas . . .
You're not just any girl.
You're Eva, Evita, Perón.
It's midnight.
How does it feel?

**Maia**
Dark.

**Director**
How does it smell?

> *maia feels the room around her.*

**Maia**
Uhm like . . . Wine?

**Director**
You should be asleep . . .
Why are you still awake?!

**Maia**
Uh . . . Uh . . .
Because.
Because I'm . . . Praying!

**Director**
Praying for what?

*almost too quickly.*

**Maia**
For my mom not to walk into my room.

**Director**
Why?

**Maia**
Because . . . I ugh—Because I'm scared.

**Director**
Scared of what?

*silence.*

**Director**
Say it.

**Maia**
I . . . I don't know.

**Director**
*(whispering into her ear)*
Don't leave me hanging here!
*(then back into the room)*
Say it!

**Maia**
I want to speak with my dad!

**Director**
Your dad? Where's your dad?

**Maia**
I don't know but I want to see him.

**Director**
What if I tell you that your dad is on the other side of the door? He's just beyond the wall. And he's looking for you. This is your last chance to speak to him.
Because tonight you're leaving home.

**Maia**
I am?

**Director**
Yes! Yes! You're packing up and moving to the big city.
Because you're aiming higher.
You're not just an actor. You're a star.
A *figure*. An *idol*.
You'll meet the pope!

*maia is getting into this now.*

**Maia**
I'll meet the pope!

**Director**
You swing open the door and you face your father down!

**Maia**
Papá!

**Director**
Yes! Now speak!

*ring.*

*a glitch between worlds.*

**Nurse Elsa**
Maia! Phone time!

**Maia**
Oh . . . now?

*ring.*

**Nurse Elsa**
Ten minutes!

**Director**
Speak to him!

**Maia**
Pa . . . ?

*ring.*

*lights shift.*

*enter father, a somber man*

*and his translator, playing tennis.*

**Father / Translator**
MAGA!

**Maia**
Pa?
Estas ahí?
*(Dad? Are you there?)*

**Father**
Make Argentina Great Again. JAJA!
Bueno Nena ¿Que pasó?

**Maia**
Necesito ayuda!
*(I need help!)*

**Father**
¿Necesitás plata?

**Translator**
Do you need money?

**Maia**
No, no, no, solo quería, no sé ch, ch, ch charlar.
*(No, no, no, I just wanted to, I don't know, ch, ch, chat.)*

                                        *he speaks right over her.*

**Father**
¿Qué te pasa?

**Father**
What's wrong?

**Maia**
Estoy ehm, estoy un poco ansiosa / y te llamaba porque—
*(I'm—ehm, I'm a bit anxious / and I was calling because—)*

**Father**
Ansiosa!? ¿Porqué?
Anxious!? Why?

**Maia**
No sé pero no me deja dormir entonces fui a ver a
un . . . psiquiatra.
*(I don't know but I can't sleep, so I went to see a . . . psychiatrist.)*

**Father**
Psiquiatra? NO! No, no, no, no.
Psiquiatras nunca Maia!

**Translator**
Psychiatrists? NO! No, no, no, no.
Never psychiatrists Maia!

**Dad**
Te van a tratar a convencer de que estás loca.
Y ya tenés el gen de tu madre,
Tenés que tener cuidado,

**Translator**
All they're good for is convincing you that you're crazy.
You've already got your mother's genes, so . . . you've got to be careful.

**Dad**
¿Pero pensás que estás loca?
Pero no podés pensar así.
Un desperdicio.

**Translator**
Do you think you're crazy?
You can't think like that.
What a waste that would be.

**Maia**
Papa—

**Dad**
Te lo digo porque te adoro,
Y porque veo tu potencial,
Tu mama tambien es brillante como vos,
Pero no dejes que eso te juege en contra.

**Translator**
I'm telling you because I adore you.
And because I see your potential.
But don't let that play against you.
Your mom is brilliant, like you.

**Father**
Y acordate siempre: de tal palo, tal astilla.

**Translator**
And always remember: the apple doesn't fall far from the tree.

> *maia casts a spell.*
> *lights shift.*
> *we're back at the ward.*
> *maia is in akila's room.*

**Akila**
—it was really pissing me off because this was his idea. And when we both went to the doctor, he got his results the same day. And it said he was fine.

**Maia**
But yours?

**Akila**
It takes longer for girls.

**Maia**
Right.

**Akila**
My results hadn't come in. And he's stubborn because he's a boy, so when he heard back from the doctors that his test was fine, I think he just assumed I was the problem.
He stopped responding to me. I told him I was waiting to hear back, that he had to be patient, but from one day to the other, he went from I love you, you'll be the best mother in the world to . . .
Literally nothing, no answer
I texted so many times and nothing.
Every time I got a text I thought it was from him but nothing.
Days went by and nothing.
I couldn't think about anything else.
One day I came back from school and his profile didn't show up anymore on my TikTok.

**Maia**
No . . .

**Akila**
He blocked me.

**Maia**
And then..?

**Akila**
I don't know . . .

Because now my phone's gone.

> *meanwhile in jacob and eduardo's room.*

**Jacob**
I know she knows.
I know she knows because of the way she looks at me sometimes. Like she'll catch me staring at her. But I'm not staring at her, I just . . . I've got nothing else to do! But she'll catch me staring and—
He stops, glancing over at Eduardo.

> *Silence. Eduardo doesn't react.*

**Jacob**
Maybe I'm staring too much?
What do you think?
Jacob looks to Eduardo for a reaction.
Nothing.

> *they seem to have an unseen, unheard language.*

**Jacob**
Yeah . . . You're right. She knows. Maybe I should just tell her then. Maybe I will tell her. But I can't just say it. That would be lame. I have to do something special.
Make something.
Maybe I'll make something?

> *He looks to Eduardo.*
> *The smallest of a small thumbs up.*
> *Back to the girls.*

**Maia**
The only thing that's wrong is that he made you feel like you did something wrong. Because you didn't. And I think it's because he was afraid. He was afraid of committing.

**Akila**
I don't wanna talk about it anymore.

**Maia**
OK.
Sorry.

*silence.*

**Akila**
Well don't just sit there.
Do something.

**Maia**
Like what?

**Akila**
Something fun.

**Maia**
Fun? Um . . . OK would you rather . . .
Would you rather make out with a sewer rat or bathe in a tub with cocoroaches?

**Akila**
"Cocoroaches!"? What's that? Neither! OK my turn.
Would you rather . . . get out of here right now but you'll never be in a movie ever in your life OR stay here for 7 years and then come out and get cast in the biggest movie of your dreams?

**Maia**
Oh shit, FUCK.
Uhhhhh, I guess, yeah 7 years in here and then big movie.

**Akila**
What?!!! That's wild.

**Maia**
I mean, It's all I ever wanted, so I guess it's worth it.
I'd get over it.

**Akila**
Oh your life out there must really suck then.

**Maia**
No, it doesn't suck! It's just—

**Akila**
Is that why you're here?

**Maia**
No.

*ring.*

**Akila**
Tell me.

*ring.*

**Akila**
What? You don't trust me?

*ring.*

**Joey**
Hi Maia, it's Joey. I have Tina on the line for you.

*maia has no idea what he's talking about.*

**Maia**
You have who on the what?

**Joey**
Tina? Just one sec.

**Maia**
Who's Tina?

*the sound of furious typing.*

**Maia**
Uh . . . Hello?
Tina?!

**Joey**
No . . . still Joey here. Just one sec.

*more furious typing.*

**Maia**
What is that sound..? I don't—

**Joey**
You've got Maia.

> *suddenly a manic woman runs on, laughing her face off.*

**Agent**
Hahaha! Oh my god!
Did someone say GOOD NEWS?!

> *click. joey walks off and . . .*
> *the agent latches onto maia like a giant squid.*

**Maia**
What?

**Agent**
Great news!
Good news . . .

**Maia**
Who are you?

**Agent**
It's Tina!
We talk all the time!

**Maia**
We do?

**Agent**
Whenever there's work involved.
I'm your agent!

**Maia**
Oh. Tina . . .
I don't think I know you.

**Agent**
I've just been so busy with pilot season—
Easter—

Spring Break—
Summer in the Bahamas—
Telluride—
Sundance—
Paris—
Cannes—
June—
It's been so hard for me to stay in touch.
Let's have a quick chat?
Does now work?
Now.

**Maia**
Uh. OK. Yeah.
Are you new or?

**Agent**
I'm on the team.
There's a whole team of us.
We'll be friends in no time.
You signed the papers, we signed you.
Ha ha! Oh my god . . .
Wow, you've been making great progress.
I think this could be your year.
Have you seen your Star Meter?
It's taking off like the fourth of July.
The Fire Department called, they said Hollywood's burning!
Whoops! That's just my favorite client. She's on *fire* . . .
Haha! Oh my god! Oh my god.
But seriously—Seriously.
Where was I?

**Maia**
Uh . . . Good news?

**Agent**
GREAT NEWS!

> *she takes maia by the shoulders, pushing her*
> *into the spotlight.*

**Agent**
You've been cast in the role of Eva Perón.
Wow . . . *Evita*!

**Maia**
Wait. Are you sure?

**Agent**
Pfff! Of course I'm sure
I mean, we just spoke to them on—Uh . . .
When did we speak to them?
Joey? JOEY!?!?

> *joey, who's been silently sitting on the other line,*
> *peeks his head out.*

**Joey**
We heard from them this morning.

**Agent**
That's right.
They called us this morning.
This is my job.
I'm your agent.
We talk all the time!
Whenever there's work involved.

**Maia**
But, who told you?

**Agent**
Hollywood's a small town, chica.
Everyone's talking about it.
You're gonna be a star.
Wow, I love good news.

> *agent exits.*
>
> *lights shift.*
>
> *we're back at the youth ward.*

*jacob paces the perimeter of the recreation room, muttering rhythmically to himself.*

*akila inspects eduardo who's sitting next to her, staring into the void.*

*maia watches from a corner.*

**Akila**
Hey Eduardo, what's your favorite movie?

*silence. eduardo doesn't react.*

*jacob continues pacing and muttering to himself.*

**Akila**
Hey Eduardo, what's your favorite song?!

*silence. eduardo doesn't react.*

**Jacob**
Leave him alone.

**Akila**
Well, you're not talking to me, so I need someone to talk to. I'm bored.
Hey Eduardo, do you like boys or girls?!

*jacob sucks his teeth.*

**Jacob**
Just leave him alone.

*eduardo doesn't react.*

**Akila**
What are *you* even doing anyways?

**Jacob**
I'm working.

**Akila**
On what?

**Jacob**
It's *private*.

**Akila**
You're all so boring.

*akila rolls her eyes.*

*maia approaches.*

**Maia**
Hey . . . excited about the Oscars tonight?

**Akila**
That's tomorrow.

**Maia**
Oh. Right.
I think I'm losing track of time.

**Akila**
It happens.

**Maia**
Right.

*maia sits next to her.*

**Maia**
Do they have any games in here?

**Akila**
No phone. No Roblox. No fun.

**Maia**
What about real games?
You guys ever play real games?

*akila stares at her like "huh".*

Like Monopoly?
Scrabble?

. . .

Bagamon?

*jacob and akila look at each other and cackle.*

**Jacob and Akila**
(*in unison*) WHAT?!

**Akila**
JINX! 123, you can't speak!

**Jacob**
/123! No!

**Akila**
I said it first!

**Jacob**
What?! No you—

**Akila**
You can't speak!

**Jacob**
But—

**Akila**
You *can't* speak.
I can't hear you.
Unless someone unlocks you.

> *she walks away*
> *and begins to laugh to herself.*
>
> *jacob gestures towards eduardo.*
>
> *then remembers eduardo doesn't speak.*

**Jacob**
Great . . .

**Akila**
Shhh!

> *jacob gestures at maia.*
>
> *maia doesn't understand.*

**Jacob**
(*muttering*)
Just say my name.

**Akila**
Did you hear something?

**Maia**
"Jacob..?"

**Jacob**
THANK FUCKING GOD!!!

**Maia**
Oh! It's a game!

**Akila**
No it's not.

**Maia**
Well I know another one where you don't have to speak!
It's called charades!

**Jacob**
Sha-who?!

**Akila**
I don't know what that is.

**Maia**
Charades?

**Akila**
No.

**Jacob**
Sounds dumb.

**Maia**
Seriously?
No, guys, it's fun. It's like an acting game.
You have to like act things out, but you can't speak.
It's like homework for actors!

**Jacob**
Homework?! Hell no.

**Maia**
No. Just—Look.
Who am I?

>*maia starts "doing" nurse elsa.*

**Akila**
Uhh . . . a grandma?

**Maia**
No!

**Akila**
You?

**Maia**
What? No!

>*maia "takes note".*

**Akila**
Taylor Swift?

>*maia breaks character.*

**Maia**
No.

**Jacob**
Oh. It's Nurse Elsa!! Duh!

**Maia**
Yes!

**Maia**
Okay you win.

>*jacob and akila do their secret handshake in celebration.*

Now you go next!

**Jacob**
What?
Ughhhh.
No, I'm busy.

**Maia**
Come on! It's fun.

**Jacob**
No.

**Akila**
Do it!

**Jacob**
Ugh. OK . . .

*jacob spins around . . . becoming.*

**Friend B**
Oh my god!
Hi Bitch!!!!!!

**Maia**
The night I entered the youth ward,
I felt a hole of emptiness in my chest.
I tried to fill it. But it only got worse.

*lights shift.*
*enter friends.*

*we're in a loud club.*

**Friend A**
Wait, what are you doing here?!!!

**Maia**
Oh! Hey! Nothing! Nothing!

*lights shift.*

*we're in a dark space.*

*the ensemble suddenly snaps into position around maia. throughout the scene, they will speak out maia's inner monologue like some twisted version of a greek chorus.*

**Ensemble**
WHAT DO I SAY?
LOOK BUSY, LOOK BUSY, LOOK BUSY.

*lights shift.*
*back to the club.*

*the ensemble take back their positions as the "friends."*

**Maia**
Just left a really terrible date.

**Friend A**
Ooooh . . . with who?

**Maia**
With this random American dude,
Who like . . . the water doesn't reach all the way to his tank, you know?

*maia points to her head.*

*an awkward silence.*
*nobody has any idea what she's talking about.*

**Ensemble**
THEY'RE NOT LAUGHING. WHY ARE THEY NOT
LAUGHING? DID THEY NOT GET IT? THEY DON'T
GET MY JOKE? AM I NOT FUNNY?!
QUICK! CHANGE THE SUBJECT.
CHANGE THE SUBJECT!

**Maia**
Anyways, you guys ready for showcase?
Showcase is coming!

*They ignore her.*
*Scrolling their phones.*

**Friend C**
Oh my god.
I just started *intermittent fasting* and I feel like my insides are burning.

**Friend B**
Uh, I think that's just hunger babe . . .

**Friend D**
Wait! Did you guys see they're remaking the Evita movie? WTF!

**Friend B**
FLOP! Why would they do that?!

**Friend C**
Straight to streaming.

**Friend A**
Who's even playing Evita?

**Friend D**
Uh . . . it doesn't say.

**Friend B**
Salma Hayek?

**Friend A**
She's gotta be a blonde.

**Friend C**
Gwyneth Paltrow?

> *the friends share a look.*
> *then turn to maia.*

**Ensemble**
GOOD MORNING GUYS, I'M GONNA TAKE YOU THROUGH MY MORNING GOOP ROUTINE.

**Friend C**
Oh my god guys, I'm really freaking out about showcase. There's always that one person who doesn't get an agent.

> *pointing at maia.*

What if it's you?!

**Maia**
What happens if you don't get an agent?

**Friend B**
You become an acting teacher.

**Friend A**
Um, this is my friend, the one I told you about?

**Friend D**
Oh my god, hi!

**Maia**
Hiiiiiiiii . . .

> *maia goes in for a kiss on the cheek.*
> *Friend D recoils.*

**Friend D**
Uhhh . . . What are you doing?

**Friend A**
She's so funny! So international!
That's just how she is!

**Friend B**
We love her . . .

**Maia**
Sorry. Was that rude? I didn't mean to.

**Friend D**
No bitch! Not at all!!!

> *shift. a dark space.*

**Ensemble**
THEY'RE LYING TO ME. THEY'RE LAUGHING AT ME.
I'M DISRESPECTFUL?! FUCK.
CAN YOU NOT SAY "WHO IS YOU" IN ENGLISH?
IS IT FUCKED UP? AM I FUCKED UP? FUCK!

> *shift. the club.*

**Friend A**
We were going to my place.
Wanna come over, drink and watch YouTube videos
until 4am?!

*shift. a dark space.*

**Ensemble**
FUCK. I LOOK LIKE SHIT.
MY HAIR IS DIRTY. FUCK.
THEY'RE LOOKING AT MY DANDRUFF.

*shift. the club.*

**Maia**
Ughhh, I don't know. I don't know.
I have to work on my Gwyneth . . .

**Friend B**
But we have coke . . .

*shift. a dark space.*

**Ensemble**
OH SHIT BITCH.
THERE'S NO TURNING BACK NOW.
WHERE DO I SIT.
NO. DON'T. DON'T TALK TO ME.

*shift. the club.*

**Friend D**
So . . . you're an actor too?

**Maia**
Yes . . .

**Friend A**
"HEY SIRI! PLAY OLIVIA RODRIGO OR SOMETHING!"

*siri's voice through a speaker.*

**SIRI**
OK. Now playing Olivia Newton-John.

**Friend C**
You guys would get along so well.
I talk about you so much!

**Maia**
Oh really? What do you say about me?

**Friend D**
Let's do a line. EVERYONE DO A LINE WITH ME!

**Friend B**
YES!!!!!!!

**Ensemble**
*SNIFFFFFF!!!!*

**Friend C**
So . . . do you live here?

**Maia**
I do! I love New Haven!

> *shift. a dark space.*

**Ensemble**
I HATE NEW HAVEN.

> *shift. the club.*

**Friend A**
Wait . . . you look so good!
Like so glowy, so much healthier . . .

**Maia**
Really?

> *shift. a dark space.*
> *psychotic laughter.*

**Ensemble**
YES. LOOK AT YOU.
YOU'RE A GODDESS.
POWER. STATUS. COCAINE!

*shift. the club.*

**Friend A**
YES!

**Friend D**
I've been working out so much.
And I've been feeling so much better / it's crazy—

**Friend B**
Wait. The Lea Michele / interview—

**Friend D**
Like working out is ACTUALLY / good for you—

**Friend B**
You guys! SHUT UP!
Did you see the Lea Michele interview?!
I can't believe she said that about Jonathan Groff.

**Friend C**
About her vag?
I know, she's soooo unhinged!

**Friend A**
Did you see it?

**Maia**
Uh . . . Yeah! She's crazy.

*shift. a dark space.*

**Ensemble**
WHO'S LEA MICHELE?!
WHO EVEN IS LEA MICHELE?!

*shift. the club.*

**Friend D**
So . . . what have you been in?
Have I seen you in anything?

*shift. a dark space.*
*psychotic laughter.*

**Emsemble**
I'LL NEVER RESPOND TO A DUMB QUESTION LIKE
THAT! IGNORANCE! IGNORANCE!
WE KILL ALL THE CATERPILLARS
AND THEN COMPLAIN THAT THERE ARE
NO BUTTERFLIES.

**Friend A**
Can I tell you something?

**Maia**
Yes.

**Friend A**
But you have to promise you won't say anything.

**Friend C**
HEY SIRI SHUT UP!!!!

**Friend D**
I'm in . . . .
The final round for . . .
The WICKED MOVIE!!!

**Friend B**
Oh. MY. GOD!

*the ensemble cheers.*

**Maia**
Can I have more coke?

*lights shift. friends exit.*

*maia, now alone, does huge lines of coke all to herself . . .
with each sniff, the world slowly shifts until . . .*

*we're back at the youth ward.
it's early morning and everyone looks hungover.*

**Nurse Elsa**
It's a bright new day . . .
You guys know the drill.
Goal and offering.

Who wants to go first?

> *silence.*

**Nurse Elsa**
Anyone? What about goop, Maia?

**Maia**
What did you just say?

**Nurse Elsa**
What about you, Maia?

> *jacob suddenly stands up.*

**Jacob**
Okay fuck it.
I've been working on this.
And I think—
Yeah I just wanted to share this.
I've been working on it for a while and . . .
It's called . . . "Nuts."

> *he clears his throat.*

**Jacob**
(*rapping*)
I'm a nutty nut, but that ain't no surprise
Living in this ward, our sanity flies
I'm spitting rhymes, feeling like the man.
Fifteen years old, king of this nutty land
They call me the "Top Nut" in this place
Got my own style, my own nutty grace
Slinging jokes, making people chuckle, ha ha
I'm a comedian, ready to hustle, brah brah
I'm nutty like a squirrel, always on the go
Making ya'll laugh, you know I crack those jokes,
But deep down inside, I'm missing the outside
I said deep down inside, I'm missing the outside
In this nutty world, I'm searching for connection
Beyond these walls, hoping for a reflection

But in this psych ward, I found a different kind of kin
People who get me, where true bonds begin
We may be a bit loony, but we're family, tight-knit
Sharing laughter even through the darkest shit
We're our own support, built a circle of trust
Laughing and supporting, we're supportive nuts
So, while my father's chasing bets, I found a family here
With the Suicide Squad I got nothing to fear

*nurse elsa looks concerned.*

**Nurse Elsa**
Uh . . .

**Jacob**
So, that's my rap, a mix of comedy and truth
With the Suicide Squad I found my groove—
Suicide, suicide,
suicide, suicide—

*nurse elsa gets up, clapping her hands.*

**Nurse Elsa**
OK! Jacob!
I'm gonna—

**Jacob**
I wasn't done!

**Nurse Elsa**
That's enough! No.
We just uh . . . We can't say those things, Jacob.

**Jacob**
Oh what . . . ? Suicide?!

**Nurse Elsa**
Jacob. Don't!

**Jacob**
SUIIIIIIIICIIIDE!

**Nurse Elsa**
You want me to call for backup? I'm calling for backup.

**Jacob**
SUUUUICIIIIDE!!!!

**Nurse Elsa**
OK. Guess what? No TV tonight!
Sorry everyone. You've just lost TV privileges because Jacob can't be cooperative.

*this lands like a bomb in the room.*

**Akila**
But the Oscars are tonight . . .

**Nurse Elsa**
I said no TV.
You've lost your TV privileges.

**Akila**
But I didn't say anything!
We didn't say anything! It was him!

**Jacob**
What?!

**Nurse Elsa**
Sorry. Consequences are consequences.

**Akila**
Jacob! You idiot!

**Jacob**
WHAT THE FUCK?!!!
ARE YOU FUCKING KIDDING ME?

**Nurse Elsa**
JACOB! Watch your tone!

**Jacob**
Oh shut the fuck up!

**Nurse Elsa**
JACOB!

**Jacob**
You're not even a real doctor!
You're just a security guard with like—drugs in your pocket/

**Nurse Elsa**
ENOUGH!

**Akila**
Shut up!

**Maia**
You're making it worse . . .

**Akila**
You're fucking everything up.

**Jacob**
You. You.
You keep talking about how much you want to kill yourself?!
Then just fucking do it!

**Maia**
Whoa! Hey!

**Nurse Elsa**
I need backup in the recreation room!

**Maia**
Don't say that!

**Jacob**
Ohhhhhhhh . . . and YOU?!!!!
(*To Maia.*)
You . . . You're just a fucking rich girl from Yale
who had a bad day!!

*eduardo laughs.*

*lights shift.*

> *maia slaps the air in front of her, dispelling an intrusive thought and yelling . . .*

**Maia**
WASABI!

> *the ensemble exits.*
>
> *total darkness.*
>
> *maia walks into a spotlight.*
>
> *she slaps the air in front of her.*

**Maia**
WASABI!
Something in Akila has changed.
She's ignoring everyone, including me: Her Buffon.
WASABI!
The doctor stopped showing up.
The medication they're giving me isn't helping me sleep, it only makes me dizzy.
And my showcase is next week.
It's my one shot, and if I miss my one shot then—
WASABI!

They brought in a new girl today.

> *enter blonde bitch in the dark.*
> *she stalks behind maia like a*
> *shadow self, a specter.*

**Maia**
"Blonde Bitch"
She's in "transit."
Whatever that means.
She looks . . . older.
Like she could be my age.
She watches me from across the room. Sizing me up.
I feel cornered.
Like she has something against *me* personally.
She walked up to me at breakfast and said—

**Blonde Bitch**
You like coffee as much as I do . . .

**Maia**
Yeah, it's the closest thing to a cigarette you can find here.

**Blonde Bitch**
Oooh. You smoke?
I thought I was the only pretty girl that smoked.
What do you smoke?

**Maia**
"Marlboro Reds."

**Blonde Bitch**
Oh come on, you can do better than that!

**Maia**
I think she thinks she's an actor.
In group meeting she said:

**Blonde Bitch**
Ugh I feel stupid and contagious!

**Maia**
That's a Nirvana song.

**Blonde Bitch**
I know. But I can make people believe anything I say.

**Maia**
In front of the nurses she's so nice it's scary.

**Blonde Bitch**
I love this place
And I love everyone here.

**Maia**
But when the nurses aren't watching.

**Blonde Bitch**
Hey!
You might win the Tony . . . But I'll win the fucking Oscar!

**Maia**
WASABI!

> *exit blonde bitch.*

**Psychiatrist**
Who are you speaking to, Maia?

> *lights shift.*
>
> *enter director and psychiatrist.*
>
> *maia spins around, disoriented, lost.*

**Director**
Water? Diet Coke? Anything?

**Psychiatrist**
Are you still hearing voices?

> *as before, they slowly encroach on maia emerging from the shadows and surrounding her from both sides.*

**Maia**
What? No.

**Psychiatrist**
Invasive thoughts?

**Maia**
When can I go outside?

**Director**
No. I need you to look inside, and be really honest with me.

**Psychiatrist**
The way you're feeling is a huge part of the process . . .

**Director**
That way I can be honest with you.

**Psychiatrist**
Can you describe these voices?

**Director**
Giving life to Eva inside you is . . .

**Psychiatrist**
Are they familiar? Are they telling you to . . . do things?

**Director**
More than just learning lines. You've got to feel her!

**Maia**
I don't think you understand me.

**Psychiatrist**
No.
Trust me.
We've read your file.
We've looked at the reports.
If you're here . . .
then it's because—

**Director**
I saw that thing in your eyes.
That desperation.

**Maia**
I need to see the light!

**Director**
Yes!

**Maia**
No.

**Psychiatrist**
OK . . .

**Maia**
Like outside!
I haven't seen the sun in days!

**Psychiatrist**
The nurses said you haven't been eating? Is that right?

**Director**
I don't want to get into the weight conversation.
but . . . Young Evita is going to need to look . . .
a little bit, uhm?
Malnourished.

**Maia**
What?!

**Psychiatrist**
Over the last two weeks.
On a scale of 1 to 10.
How often have you been bothered
by any of the following symptoms:
Little interest or pleasure in doing things?

**Maia**
There's nothing to do.

**Director**
We need you to find pleasure
because this is a story about love, about leadership
tenacity and *pasión*.
I cast you because I saw someone with . . .

**Psychiatrist**
Depression? Feelings of hopelessness?

**Maia**
I need to get out!
My showcase is next week!

**Director**
. . . access to deeper parts of their soul!
Someone who can crack themselves open.
Someone willing to give it all.
Vulnerable, unfiltered, raw.
I picked you because I thought you'd be the one—

**Psychiatrist**
. . . to 10, Maia.
I need a number.

**Maia**
I just—

**Psychiatrist**
Acting sounds stressful . . . is that really what you need?

**Maia**
Yes! I need to be in the American movies!

**Psychiatrist**
OK . . .

**Director**
I love that passion!

**Maia**
You can't take this away from me.

**Psychiatrist**
When did your mother first start exhibiting these symptoms?

**Maia**
No, that's not what I meant.

**Director**
You do look a bit . . . swollen.

**Psychiatrist**
Maybe a slight increase . . .

**Maia**
What's my diagnosis? Like with all these questions . . . what's my actual diagnosis?

**Psychiatrist**
The nurses told me you were a bit nervous after a phone call with your mother?

**Director**
She knew what real pain felt like . . .

**Maia**
I don't wanna go back to Argentina!

**Psychiatrist**
Just answer the question Maia.
Does the phone make you anxious?

**Maia**
Yes obviously, all the time!

**Director**
Time plays a huge part in my film!
Precisely because Eva didn't have any, you know?

**Psychiatrist**
Feeling that you'd be better off dead or thoughts of hurting yourself?

**Director**
I need you to imagine what it would be like to die
as young as she did.

*maia collapses.*

*lights shift.*

*we're back at the ward.*

*maia rocks back and forth, softly,
akila watches her.*

*annoyed by the sound.*

**Maia**
(*quietly to herself*)
*Good morning guys, I'm gonna take you through my morning goop routine.*
*Good morning guys, I'm gonna take you through my morning goop routine.*
*Good morning guys/*

**Akila**
Ughh . . .

**Maia**
What?

**Akila**
Do you realize that you're always talking to yourself..?
Like . . . everyone can hear you.

**Maia**
I'm . . . I'm just doing my homework.

*akila looks at maia like she's crazy.*

**Akila**
Homework..?

**Maia**
Everything can be homework when you're an actor.

**Akila**
That's so dumb.

*maia shoots up.*

**Maia**
So you're not mad at me?

**Akila**
Why would I be mad at you?

**Maia**
It's just you've been ignoring me for . . .
I don't know how many days.
I thought you were mad.

**Akila**
No . . . I'm mad at Jacob.
Because he's a stupid idiot.

**Maia**
I'm sure he didn't mean to—

**Akila**
I'm mad at Nurse Elsa.
Because we missed the Oscars.

**Maia**
Well, yeah. I get that.

**Akila**
I'm even mad at Eduardo!

**Maia**
What? Why?

**Akila**
Just because!
I'm just mad.
I'm not mad at you.
I'm just mad.

*maia gets up.*
*she searches the room.*
*then hands akila a TV remote.*

**Maia**
Here. Pick a channel.

**Akila**
What?

**Maia**
Just pick a channel. Like a TV.

*maia gestures her to click on it.*

**Akila**
But there's no TV time anymore. Remember?

**Maia**
We can watch whatever we want.

*akila is sort of weirded out about it.*
*she clicks the remote.*

**Maia**
Hello everyone! I'm Carlita Montini and this is your
7 o'clock news. Mind-blowing reports out of the town

of Encantito this evening: locals are reporting strange occurrences surrounding a mysterious figure known only as "Bruno". But here's the catch, folks: Nobody wants to talk about Bruno.

*eduardo perks up.*

*jacob tries his best to ignore her.*

*akila changes channel.*

**Maia**
(*Maria's version of the National Anthem*)
Oh lord can't you see . . . Up the north . . .

*akila changes channel*

**Maia**
Vive en una piña debajo del mar! Bob! Esponja!

*eduardo gets excited.*
*he likes this song.*

*so does akila.*

*jacob still plays it cool but we can tell he wants to laugh.*

**Maia**
Su cuerpo absorbe y sin estallar . . . Bob! Esponja!
El mejor amigo que podrías desear Bob! Esponja!
Bob! Esponja! Bob! Esponja!
El es Bob! ESPONJA!

*akila changes channel.*

**Maia**
The five men nominated for this category have shown inhuman depths of empathy. We've seen them cry like no other men before, we've seen them speak like no other men before and deliver monologues so deep and profound and . . . And the Oscar goes to . . .

*a beat.*

*a drum roll.*

**Maia**
EDUARDO!

> *eduardo jumps up in excitement.*
>
> *he does a series of uncontrollable physical movements that become a dance.*
>
> *it's eduardo's moment.*
>
> *nurse elsa walks in but they ignore her.*
>
> *she takes note.*
>
> *but they ignore her.*
>
> *after a moment, eduardo spins.*
>
> *lights shift.*
>
> *eduardo pulls a baseball cap out of his pocket and becomes . . .*

**Director**
OK quiet on set! Quiet on set!
We're gonna start off with the last scene.

> *we're on set.*
>
> *enter ensemble as crew members, setting up the shot.*

**Maia**
The balcony scene?

**Director**
Yeah.
What? Is there a problem?

**Maia**
No. No.
I'm just gonna take a second to get into the zone.

> *maia runs her key phrase.*

**Maia**
Good morn—
Good morning guys—
Morn—

**Director**
Let's just get moving.
We'll shoot a series. OK?
Roll sound.
And . . . GOOP!

> *the ensemble stands in position.*
>
> *a spotlight on maia.*
> *the footage is rolling.*

**Maia**
What did you say?

> *lights shift.*
>
> *the ensemble is just a crew again.*

**Director**
I said ACTION!
Alright let's go! Let's go!
We're losing light.

> *maia begins to sing don't cry for me argentina.*

**Director**
Wait wait wait.
What are you doing?
We cut the song!

**Maia**
Oh we did?

**Director**
Yes. We're not doing a musical here.
We're just doing the speech. Let's go! Let's move.
And . . . ACTION!

**Maia**
(*in a thick Gwyneth accent*)
Compañeros!
Recently in the hours of my illness,
I have thought often of this message from my heart.
Who am I?

**Director**
Cut! Cut!
What are you saying?
What's that accent you're doing?
It's weird, just . . . don't.

> *the crew sets up the next shot.*

**Maia**
OK. OK. Should I try something else? I can—

**Director**
Just do your natural accent.
That's what I like.

**Maia**
You got it!

**Director**
Here's a word: *authentic*. Right?

**Maia**
Yeah.

**Director**
That's what we need. OK?
Let's roll sound!
Picture up! And . . . ACTION!

**Maia**
Compañeros!
Recently in the hours of my illness,
I have thought often of this message from my heart—

> *ring.*

> *the lights shift. ring.*
>
> *enter joey and agent. ring*

**Joey**
Hey Maia, it's Joey.
I've got Tina on the line for you.

**Maia**
Oh hi!!! Is everything / okay?

> *tina, the agent, emerges.*

**Agent**
/ Hey Maia!
How are ya?

**Maia**
Hiiii . . . Good!
How's—

**Agent**
Listen, I'm driving into the hills here, so if I lose you,
I might—*(static sound)*
OK?

**Maia**
Uh . . . Yeah that's OK. That's OK.
So, what's up? How's everything?

**Agent**
I'm good.
I'm good.
Um . . .
Look. I got a call from Eric.
What's happening on set?
He gave me a quick rundown.

**Maia**
Oh yeah?
What'd he say?

**Agent**
He mentioned you're having trouble with an accent?

**Maia**
No. No. I just—
He—he—
He wants me to do this like really basic
Like stereotypical thing? Right? But I just
I feel like it could be so much better
If it was more real. You know?

**Agent**
Well he is the Director . . . so . . . You know?
That's not to say you can't—*(static garbled sounds!)*
But you need—*(static garbled sounds!)*

**Maia**
Uh . . . Tina? You're—

**Agent**
*(Static sounds!)*

**Maia**
You're breaking down—Sorry, I mean breaking up!

**Agent**
*(Static sounds!)*—Because your opinions are just opinions
but his opinions are professional opinions, right?
So I would just try it his way.
Give it a shot.
Be open.
Be open.

*lights shift.*
*the ensemble sets up the next shot.*

**Director**
Listen, she gave this speech in front of one million
people right after she was diagnosed with
terminal cancer, right? I need you to really go there.
Show me the blood. OK? Show me the fear.

**Maia**
OK. I can do that.

**Director**
Great and the uhm . . .
The ACCENT? What's going on there?
It doesn't really sound Argentinean, does it?
It's kind of bourgeois. Like, French or something.

**Maia**
I mean I'm Argentinean.
That's actually how I speak.

**Director**
British kind of. Or maybe Russian?
Just try leaning into a more Latin American sound.
Because right now it's kind of unplaceable.

**Maia**
This is my voice,
You want authentic,
This *is* authentic.

**Director**
You know what I'm talking about,
Let's not overcomplicate this . . .
Let's roll sound please!
Picture up! And . . . ACTION!

**Maia**
COMPAÑEROS!!!
Recently in the hours of my illness I have thought often of this message
from my heart . . . Who am I?
Am I?
Am I?
Am . . . I . . . ?
WASABI!

*maia casts a spell*
*dispelling the film set.*

**Maia**
WASABI!
WASABI!
WASABI!
WASABI!
WASABI!
WASABI!
WASABI!!!

*lights shift.*
*we're back at the ward.*
*darkness.*
*akila in her room*
*she hums a song while playing with a ball.*
*enter maia, cautiously.*

**Maia**
Psss! Hey!

**Akila**
What are you doing?

**Maia**
Nothing. I can't sleep.

**Akila**
Me neither.

**Maia**
Did you uhm—
Hear—
About uhm . . .

**Akila**
You got discharged.

**Maia**
No.
It's uhm—
About Jacob.

**Akila**
What about him?

**Maia**
He . . . tried to kill himself.

**Akila**
How?

**Maia**
Swallowed a battery.

**Akila**
Wow.
He wanted to die but instead he got a recharge.

*beat.*

**Akila**
It's a joke.

**Maia**
Yeah, I know.

*beat.*

**Akila**
People think killing yourself is easy
Because movies make it like look easy
But it's not.
It actually requires a LOT of logistical planning.
And that's what I'm bad at.
Like I'm really good at *wanting* to die,
I'm just really bad at organizing it.

*maia stifles a laugh.*

**Akila**
What? I'm being serious.

**Maia**
I know.
I'm sorry, I'm listening.

**Akila**
Last time I tried to kill myself, I was at home, my parents were both at work so it was perfect and I was *so* ready.

I had like made the decision.

I wrote this long ass letter with specific instructions on how to take good care of my dog. I locked the doors, put some music on, went to my mom's bathroom and took an entire bottle of Tylenol.

But guess what?

My mom keeps her *laxatives* hidden in Tylenol bottles because she doesn't want my dad to find out that she's addicted to laxatives. I'm not even exaggerating . . . It was fucking humiliating. There was no car at home and my mom had confiscated my credit card so I couldn't get an Uber and so I had to take the bus to the hospital.

The BUS.

People kept staring at me because I smelled so bad. And then I got to the hospital and tried to lie and say that I had just taken a bunch of laxatives because I wanted to do a colon cleanse but obviously they didn't believe me, and so they pumped my stomach and like next thing I know they brought me here!
Again! And—

*maia stifles another laugh.*

**Akila**
Oh my god.
Are you laughing?!

*maia tries really hard not to laugh.*

**Maia**
No. I'm sorry that happened to you.

**Akila**
You think it's funny!

**Maia**
No I just sometimes I laugh when I'm nervous.
I don't think it's funny!

**Akila**
It's OK if you think it's funny.

**Maia**
IT'S 100 percent NOT FUNNY
THAT YOU WANT TO DIE SO BAD.
IT'S ACTUALLY FUCKED UP.

*an awkward silence. we can't tell if akila is insulted by this or not and then . . .*

*they both erupt into laughter. after a moment . . .*

**Maia**
Akila?

**Akila**
Yeah.

**Maia**
I like you. Please don't die.

*akila says nothing. then.*

**Akila**
So why are you here? Really?
I've literally told you everything about me.
And I still don't know anything about you.
Really.

**Maia**
I know, it's just—

**Akila**
What?

**Maia**
I don't know—

**Akila**
Just tell me!

**Akila**
What?!

**Maia**
I don't want to—

**Akila**
Just say it!

**Maia**
I can't—

**Akila**
Just say IT!

**Maia**
I hear voices!! Okay?

*silence.*

**Akila**
Voices . . .
Like . . . in your head?

**Maia**
It's been happening for a while.

**Akila**
For how long?

**Maia**
I guess.
When I was a kid?
Like, when I was really young.
I would stay up imagining these things.
Because I had to stay awake.

**Akila**
You *had* to?

**Maia**
Yeah. Because my mom.
She's uhm . . .
Well she's better now,
I think? But
Back then—
She was mad after my Dad left her. And I was her only way to get to him. My room was like an interrogation room.
And if I didn't respond Or said the wrong thing . . . Then it would become like a torture chamber. She would burn my scalp with a hair dryer
Or
press a pillow onto my face until—Well yeah, it got bad. And it got worse over time.
Because wine became cocaine and oh god, cocaine . . .
WASABI! *(but it's smaller than the others, quieter)*

> *beat.*

My room didn't have a lock but the bathroom did.
So I'd stay up, imagining things these voices?
To stay awake, stay alert, stay safe you know?
When I moved to America, I thought I was leaving all that behind.
That I would be able to build my own life here.
But I didn't.
Because I still couldn't sleep.
And the voices, they only got louder.
They became the voices of my parents, my teachers, my friends.
Gwyneth Paltrow.
The night I ended up at the youth ward, the voices were so loud, I couldn't shut them off.
So I ended up on the bathroom floor.
The tiles were so cold that I just wanted them on my head.
In my head?
So I started banging my head against the floor.
And this is where it all gets glitchy.
I went to the ER and tried to explain this to them,

They said they would keep me in observation for the night
and then let me go home the next day with a prescription.
But instead they just put me to sleep.
So that they could put me in an ambulance.
So that they could dress me in hospital clothes.
So that they could put me here.
And maybe they did the right thing.
Because . . . the more I talk about it the more I realize that . . .
Maybe they're right?
Maybe I should be here.
Maybe I am crazy?

*silence.*

**Akila**
The floor huh?
Can't believe I've never thought of that.
And it's been there the whole time.

*they share a glance.*
*they laugh.*

**Akila**
How come that was so hard for you to say?

**Maia**
I don't know. I've never told anyone that.

**Akila**
Do you feel better now that you did?

**Maia**
Yeah. I do . . .

*beat.*

**Maia**
Akila?
Can we be friends when we get out?
*If* we get out.

**Akila**
You could've gotten out of here days ago if you were smart.

**Maia**
What are you talking about?

**Akila**
I could've gotten out too if I had wanted to.
I just didn't want to. Not until now I guess.

**Maia**
How?

*silence.*

**Akila**
All you gotta do is *act normal. Pretend.*
You should be good at that—you're an actress, right?
You've gotta give them exactly what they want.
You've got to agree with everything they say.
You've gotta make them believe that they fixed you.
That they cured you.
That this place saved your life.
You get it?

**Maia**
Yeah. I think so.

**Akila**
If they ask if you've been improving—you say:
*Yes, absolutely.*
If they ask you:

*enter psychiatrist.*

**Psychiatrist**
How are you feeling?

**Maia and Akila**
I've never felt better.

**Psychiatrist**
Have you been eating?

**Maia and Akila**
I've never been hungrier.

**Psychiatrist**
And how's your sleep?

**Maia**
I've never slept better.

**Akila**
Because if you tell them the truth?
They'll keep you here forever.

>                             *lights shift.*
>                        *we're back on set.*
>           *maia is ready for her close up.*

**Maia**
*(in the most exaggerated stereotypical Latin American accent you've ever heard in your life)*
Compañeros!
Recently in the hours of my illness I have thought often of
this message from my heart . . . Who am I?
I will not tell you the usual lies.
I'm not important because of what I've done;
I'm not important because of what I've renounced;
I'm not important because of what I am or what I have.
I have only one thing that matters, and I have it in
my heart.
It sets my soul aflame.
It wounds my flesh and it burns in my sinews.
I won't tell you that I don't deserve this. Yes, I deserve this.
But I deserve it for one thing alone,
Which is worth more than all the gold in the world!
I deserve it for all that I've done
For the love of the people!

For my love for the people!
And for Perón!

> *lights shift.*
> *enter psychiatrist and director.*

**Director**
And . . . cut! That's it! That's the take.
That's a wrap everybody, that's a wrap!

**Maia**
That was the take?

**Psychiatrist and Director**
Yes!

**Psychiatrist**
So articulate. So clear.

**Director**
That was incredible!

> *they surround her on both sides.*

**Psychiatrist**
With the hospital over capacity, it's a miracle we managed to find you a bed here. But hey take it as a compliment, you look young!

**Maia**
Thank you.
I finally feel like myself.

**Director.**
You found your voice.

**Maia**
And that's because of you.

**Director**
Hold on to that feeling. We're going to need it again.

**Maia**
Yes and that's all because of you.

**Psychiatrist**
You're ready to be discharged.
Do you have someone picking you up?

**Maia**
So . . . that's all?

**Director and Psychiatrist**
YES!
That was . . .

**Ensemble**
Exactly what we needed from you.

> *a series of snapshots.*
> *as the ensemble cycles through all the characters*
> *and worlds of the play.*
> *maia says goodbye.*

**Ensemble**
Exactly what we imagined from you.
Exactly what we thought you were capable of.
Exactly what we want you to sound like.
Exactly what we think of you.
Exactly why we picked you.
Exactly who you're supposed to be.
Exactly what you're supposed to be doing.

> *until at the very end . . .*
> *maia is left alone.*

**Ensemble**
Exactly what we needed from you.
Exactly what we needed from you.
Exactly what we needed from you.
Exactly what we needed from you.

*we hear the columbia pictures jingle again.*

*maia walks up to the foot of the stage. all dark save for the spotlight.*

*she stares out at the audience. for as long as she feels is right and then . . .*
*she jumps, disappearing into the dark.*

**End of Play**